POET AND ARTIST
IN GREECE

SIX GREEK SCULPTORS

By Ernest A. Gardner, Litt.D.
Emeritus Professor of Archæology
in the University of London, with
81 illustrations.   Cloth, 10/- net.

POET AND ARTIST
IN GREECE

ERNEST A. GARDNER

LITT.D.

Emeritus Professor of Archæology
in the University of London

3 HENRIETTA STREET, LONDON, W.C.2

First Published 1933

Printed *in* Great Britain
By The Camelot Press Ltd
London *and* Southampton

CONTENTS

CHAP.   PAGE

PREFACE 11

I. INTRODUCTION 13

II. THE ILIAD 27

III. THE ODYSSEY 39

IV. THE EPIC CYCLE 55

V. HESIOD AND THE HOMERIC HYMNS . . 81

VI. THE LYRIC POETS 85

VII. DRAMATIC POETS 109

VIII. HELLENISTIC ART 124

LIST OF ILLUSTRATIONS

PAGE

1. Adam and Eve · · · · · · · 18
2. Departure of Amphiaraus · · · · 19
3. Helen and Paris · · · · · 21
4 { Agamemnon and Briseis · · · · 22
  { Embassy to Achilles · · · · 22
5. Pursuit of Troilus by Achilles · · · 22
6. Death of Troilus · · · · · 23
7. Neoptolemus slays Astyanax and Priam · · 24
8. Neoptolemus with head of Astyanax · · · 25
9. Separation of Ajax and Hector · · · · 30
10. Hector and Ajax exchange gifts · · · · 31
11. Achilles and Hector · · · · · 32
12. Ransom of Hector, Priam and Achilles · · 33
13. Hector and Andromache · · · · 34
14. Æneas and Ajax, Hector and Achilles · · 35
15. Helen, Paris, Hector, Andromache · · · 36
16. Fight over body of Euphorbus · · · · 37
17. Odysseus and Cyclops (Aristonous Vase) · · 40
18. Odysseus and Cyclops (Laconian Vase) · · 41
19. Circe and Odysseus · · · · · 45
20. Odysseus' ship and the Sirens · · · 46
21. Odysseus and the Sirens · · · · 47
22. Odysseus and Nausicaa · · · · 49
23. Penelope and her Loom · · · · 51
24. Odysseus and Eurycleia · · · · 52
25. Odysseus slaying the Suitors · · · 53
26. Peleus seizing Thetis · · · · · 58
27. Judgement of Paris (Hieron) · · · 60
28. The three Goddesses in their chariots · · 62
29. Achilles and Memnon.   Thetis, Eos and Scales · · 68
30. Zeus, Hermes and Scales · · · · 69

PAGE

31 { Embassy to Achilles 70
{ Sleep and Death with the Body of Sarpedon . . 70

32. Eos with the body of Memnon 71

33. Fight over the body of Achilles 72

34. Ajax and Odysseus dispute over arms of Achilles . . 73

35. Odysseus and Diomed with rival Palladia . . . 75

36. Iliupersis (Vivenzio Vase) 76

37. Infant Hermes and Cattle of Apollo 82

38. Heracles threatens the Sun-god 88

39. Danae in the Tower 89

40. Danae in the Chest 90

41. Theseus under the Sea 93

42. Theseus and Amphitrite 94

43. Crœsus on the Pyre 95

44. Exploits of Theseus 100

45. Caeneus attacked by Centaurs 104

46. Actors as Birds 110

47. Iphigenia in Taurus 111

48. Medea 113

49. Antigone 117

50. Orestes and Clytæmnestra 121

51. Orestes purified by Apollo 122

52. Sunrise (Blacas Vase) 125

SOURCES FROM WHICH ILLUSTRATIONS
ARE DERIVED

1. Wickhoff, Roman Art. Fig 1 (after Wiener Genesis).
2. Mon. X., 4–5 A.
3. Arch. Zeit. 1882, p. 3.
4. Mon. VI., 19.
5. Mon. IV., 57.
6. Mon. I., 34.
7. Gerhard, Etr. & Camp. V., 21.
8. J.H.S. XIV., ix.
9. Arch. Zeit., 1854, 67.
10. Mon. I., 35–6.
11. A.V. 204.
12. Mon. VIII., 37.
13. J.H.S. IX., iii.
14. Annali d. I. 1862, B.
15. A.V. 322.
16. Salzmann-Nécropole de Camiros, 53.
17. Mon. IX., 14.
18. Mon. I., 7.
19. J.H.S. XIII., ii.
20. Mon. I., 8.
21. J.H.S. XIII., 1.
22. A.V. 218.
23 }
24 } Mon. IX., 42.
25. Mon. X., 53.
26. A.V. 227.
27. Wiener Vorlegebl. A. 5.
28. Roscher III., p. 1618.
29. Millin Vases I., 19.
30. Mon. II., 10 B.
31. Mon. VI., 21.
32. Wiener Vorlegebl. vii.
33. Mon. I., 51.
34. Mon. VIII., 41.
35. Mon. VI., 22.
36. Baumeister XII., after Tischbein.
37. Mus. Greg, Etr., II., 83.
38. J.H.S. XIX., ix.
39 } Berlin Winckelmannspro-
40 } gram 1854.
41. J.H.S. XVIII., p. 277 (after Mus. Ital. I.).
42. J.H.S. XVIII., xiv.
43. Mon. I., 54.
44. J.H.S. Pl. X.
45. J.H.S. XVII., vi.
46. J.H.S. Pl. XIV.
47. Mon. IV., 51.
48. Arch. Zeit. 1847, 3.
49. Mon. X., 27.
50. Gerhard., Etr. & Campan. V., 24.
51. Mon. IV., 48.
52. Welcker, Alte Denkmäler III., 9.

Abbreviations used in above List

Mon.—Monumenti dell' Instituto.
Arch. Zeit.—Archiologisch Zeitung.
A.V.—Gerhard–Auslerlesene Vasenbilder.
Annali d. I.—Annali dell ' Instituto.
J.H.S.—Journal of Hellenic Studies.

References are not, as a rule, given to collections such as Baumeister's Denkmäler, but to earlier publications from which these are derived.

PREFACE

LESSING'S LAOCOÖN, published in 1766, laid down the boundaries between artistic and literary representations, and investigated the relations of the two forms of expression ; and it still remains the standard work on the subject. Much has been written since that time, and the material for the study has been greatly amplified, especially in our knowledge of the art of the vase-painter. Professor Robert's *Bild und Lied*, published in 1881, is a most valuable contribution to the study. Acknowledgement is also due to Professor Percy Gardner's *Principles of Greek Art*.

The present volume contains the substance of a course given as " the Yates Lectures " at University College, London, in 1931. These lectures were illustrated by lantern slides, of which a selection is here reproduced on a miniature scale, and may serve at least to indicate the nature of the subjects represented. Those who wish can supplement them by reference to collections such as Baumeister's *Denkmäler des Klassischen Altertums* or Gerhard's *Auslerlesene Vasenbilder*. Adequate reproductions of the style of Greek vases may be found in the magnificent plates of Furtwängler and Reichbhold's *Griechische Vasenmalerei*.

No formal index is provided, since the List of Illustrations makes it easy to refer to any subject wanted. No attempt is made at complete consistency in the spelling of Greek names. As a rule, the Latin form is used for names fairly well known to English readers, while less familiar forms are directly transliterated from the Greek.

CHAPTER I

INTRODUCTION

"A POEM is a speaking picture, a picture is a mute poem." The familiar epigram of Simonides emphasises the main distinction between the two arts, which appeal from mind to mind by the senses of hearing and of sight respectively. The relation of the two is not, however, so simple as it appears to be. For example, the appeal of a written or printed poem is sometimes to the eye rather than to the ear, although theoretically the visible symbols in this case have a conventional phonetic value. Indeed, some men are so constituted that even when they hear a word or a poem they find it easier to grasp the meaning if they visualise it. Others, especially the illiterate, learn from pictures much that they could not gather from the spoken or written word. When Horace said,

> " *Segnius irritant animos demissa per aurem*
> *Quam quæ sunt oculis subjecta fidelibus* "

(" Less keenly are our spirits stirred by what passes through the ear than by what is set before our trustworthy eyes "), he was indeed thinking of performances upon the stage ; but the statement is capable of a wider application.

Much depends also upon the purpose or aim of every communication, whether visible or audible. It is possible to classify such products as being, in the main, magical, didactic, or artistic, though many cross-divisions run through any such classification.

Some authorities think that the wonderfully realistic drawings or paintings or carvings of animals made by cave men have a magical intention – that is to say that the possession of an exact facsimile of an animal gives the man who makes it some magic power over the animal ; and that the representation of such an animal as struck by arrows or other weapons may actually lead to success on the part of the hunter.   This is a very primitive case ; but a similar conception may be seen in far more advanced art, for example in that of Egypt.   Not only are the images of the deceased in Egyptian tombs made as lifelike as possible, in order to attract the soul to them, but the possessions and offerings depicted on the wall-paintings of the tombs are intended to place those possessions at the disposal of the deceased after his death ; or, to take a quite modern instance, the advertisements with which our walls are placarded are intended to stimulate a desire for the articles advertised, and even in some cases to hypnotise, so to speak, the possible purchaser into the acquisition of such articles, and so to promote their sale.

Another very common purpose is to record facts or to tell a story.   This is most easily to be found in literary documents ; but it is also not infrequent in carved or pictorial records.   It occurs, for example, on a neolithic rock-painting in Scandinavia, which has an unmistakable representation of a sea-fight.   It is extremely common in Egyptian and Mesopotamian records, which were for the most part intended to give an exact chronicle of the victories and exploits of kings, or to record acts of worship to the gods.   In this case it was common for the relief or pictorial record to be helped out and defined by written or incised inscriptions.   The same method was taken over and extended by early Christian art, because it was peculiarly adapted to bring before the eyes of the illiterate the stories of the Bible or of the lives of the saints. In this case it clearly had a didactic character and intention. A similar purpose is served by the illustrations or diagrams added to scientific works or even to trade catalogues; these are definitely intended to help out and to make clear the things described in the text. This kind of use evidently overlaps with that of advertisements, as described above. The purpose of identifying an object or asserting ownership of it may also lead to marking it or otherwise making it recognisable. All these various purposes can be better served as artistic or technical skill comes into play. And here the decorative tendency comes to have considerable influence, and the desire for balance and symmetry. This desire is particularly visible in oriental art, and through this came to affect early art in Greece. The artistic desire to make a pleasing pattern is often prominent. Imitation of natural objects was also common from the earliest times; and such figures of animals or men, whether singly or joined together into groups, offer an opportunity for recording an event or telling a story. Such representations sometimes appeal directly to the mind of the observer, without any conscious translation into sounds or words.

The process by which drawings or pictures of objects, animate or inanimate, came to be used with a phonetic meaning is an obscure one. At the one extremity we find a system of ideographs, as in China, each symbol having a definite meaning, but different phonetic equivalents; consequently it is possible for those familiar with the system but not speaking the same language or dialect to read the same meaning into an ideograph, but to pronounce it quite differently. This is not very different in

effect from the picture chronicle ; but there is the great
difference that the individual symbols are not, as a rule,
easy to recognise from the form, but are highly conven-
tionalised.

The transition from pictographs or ideographs to a
phonetic system can be traced in various scripts ; in
Egypt and in Mesopotamia, and also probably in Crete, a
series of symbols which spells out a word phonetically may
be supplemented by a determinative, which, though
conventional in form, is yet easily recognisable as representing the object of which the name has been spelt out.
Thus the two systems practically duplicate each other.
An inversion of the same process takes place when any
person or object is represented in carving or drawing, and
its name is attached to it or inscribed upon it. Thus, on
the François vase, not only are the names of persons
written beside them, but the pitcher which Polyxena has
dropped is labelled ὑδρία (jug), and the seat on which
Priam is sitting is labelled θῶκος (seat). In such cases
the direct appeal to the eye is explained or supplemented
by the other appeal, that to the ear, though this latter is
indirect – that is to say, the visible signs must be trans-
lated into sound before they have any meaning.

The instances just quoted are of a very elementary
nature ; but the principle is the same when the exploits
of a king, carved in stone, are associated with a record of
these exploits in a conventional inscription, sometimes cut
right across the figures. In such a case the two methods of
expression are combined on a basis of equality. In other
instances the one or the other is predominant. For
example, on the chest of Cypselus, dedicated at Olympia
about 600 B.C., there was represented a whole series of
mythological scenes ; and in each scene was set a hexa-
meter verse, curling about among the figures, and stating

what was the subject represented. Such an arrangement was not common in the finest age of Greek art ; but something very like it appears in examples of the Tabula Iliaca, dating from the Hellenistic age, where a summary of the whole Iliad is inscribed on the marble, and the chief scenes of the poem are represented much as scriptural scenes are in the " Biblia Pauperum." It is, in fact, an illustrated compendium of the poem, such as might be made at the present time. But such a proceeding is not satisfactory either for the poet, whose work is cut about and abridged ; or for the artist, who is left little scope for originality or invention.

In such cases the two appeals, to the ear and to the eye, are combined. More often they are separate, and in that case, as Lessing points out, a spoken or written narrative involves extension in time, and records the sequence of actions or events. A picture or carving, on the other hand, involves extension in space, and can only represent one moment of time. When it is desired to represent a narrative or sequence of events, such as forms the usual theme of prose or poetry, the space art is at a disadvantage, and has to select from different means of expression. These have been distinguished by Wickhoff[1] as the isolating, the continuous, and the comprehensive (he calls it complementary) methods. We shall come across examples of all of these if we study the relation of poet and painter in Greece ; but it is as well to note one or two clear examples of each. The first is the commonest and simplest, and is also in accordance with the modern practice of illustrating a story. The artist in this case selected some action or position, readily recognisable and intelligible, and characteristic of the story. He represents, in fact, just what he sees before him or would see if he

---

[1] *Roman Art*, p. 13.

Bɢ

were present at the action portrayed. He has not, however, in this case any opportunity of telling what went
before or what followed after. A favourite device of early
art is therefore what is called the continuous method. In
this, a figure or figures are repeated several times in the
same picture, in successive stages of action or movement.

1. Adam and Eve

A good example is offered in a mediæval manuscript of
Genesis quoted by Wickhoff. Here the fall of Adam is
represented by three scenes, all set in a continuous
landscape. In the first, Adam and Eve stand by the tree
and take the apples, in the second they are covering their
nakedness with fig-leaves, and, in the third, they are
hiding in the bushes from the presence of God, indicated
by a hand in the sky. They are thus represented in three
successive positions, which must be separated by some
interval of time. If, instead of this, a number of quickly
succeeding positions were represented, we should have an
effect now familiar to us in the cinematograph. But even
the slower sequence is eminently suitable for representing

a story or a succession of events, and consequently was used extensively in the chronicle-reliefs of Mesopotamia and Egypt, in mediæval tales from the Bible or from the lives of saints, and in Roman reliefs like that of Trajan's column. But in modern times it is practically restricted to drawings for children or in the comic papers. A curious coincidence may be seen in a popular advertisement of a certain motor spirit and an illustration to Dante by Botticelli, quoted by Wickhoff. In both alike suddenness and surprise are expressed in the same way by a figure with two heads, one turned each way, to indicate two rapidly succeeding positions. Such devices as these,

2. Departure of Amphiaraus

however, appear not to have satisfied the artistic sensibilities of the Greeks ; at any rate they were not used by the Greeks—with some possible exceptions.

The comprehensive (or complementary) method, on the other hand, was often followed by the Greek vase-painter, and it was readily adapted to the aims and traditions of his art. In this method the same figure does not appear twice in a single picture or relief, but may be represented in such action or position as tells more than could be actually seen on the spot. The scene of the departure of Amphiaraus from his home to join the Seven against Thebes, as represented on a Corinthian vase, offers a good example of the method. In accordance with the common practice of Greek vase-painters of adapting traditional types rather than inventing new ones, the scene here is the familiar one of the departure of a warrior in a chariot, with such additions and modifications as are necessary to make it fit the story. Amphiaraus is represented as mounting his chariot, driven by his charioteer Baton, who is receiving a parting cup from an attendant. The hero looks back, as he mounts the chariot, and has a drawn sword in his hand. Behind him, in the porch of the palace, is a group of children and women, the last of them, Eriphyle, holding conspicuously in her hand an enormous necklace. The reference here is clearly to the necklace of Harmonia, with which Polynices had bribed her to send her husband on the expedition against Thebes. It is instructive to compare this rather crude representation of the necklace with Polygnotos' picture at Delphi, in which Eriphyle conceals it in the folds of her tunic. Amphiaraus is evidently thought of as having drawn his sword to punish her for her treachery ; and the other members of the family stretch out their hands towards him as if supplicating him to spare her. In front of the horses is a seated man in an attitude of dejection, probably a seer who forsees the disastrous end of the expedition. Thus the whole story is either told or hinted at – the treachery of Eriphyle, the wrath of Amphiaraus, his yielding to his family's entreaties, his departure, and the disastrous end of the expedition. It would not indeed have been likely, in the circumstances, that Eriphyle would carry the necklace in such a conspicuous way, or that Amphiaraus would actually carry a drawn sword while he mounted his chariot. But there is nothing impossible in any of the actions or positions represented, and it is conceivable, though not probable, that they should all take place contemporaneously.

It is interesting to compare this scene from the story
of Amphiaraus with its treatment by a vase-painter of the
fifth century B.C., who follows the isolating or selective
method.   In both alike the essential thing is the bribing
of Eriphyle with the necklace.   In the later representation the scene is restricted to two figures ; Polynices
holds out the necklace and Eriphyle is evidently tempted
by it.   But the treatment suggests a pedlar tempting a
lady with his goods rather than an event in a tragic
history.   It is not necessary to give other instances of the

3. Helen and Paris

comprehensive method here, because we shall come across
many examples of it in the course of our study.   But it is
interesting to note other cases in which the custom and
tradition of the vase-painter have influenced the type by
which a scene is represented.   A good example is offered
by the scheme of the marriage procession, which comes to
be adapted to express conditions so different as the
elopement of Paris and Helen and the leading away of
Briseis from Achilles.   In bridal processions the usual order
is for the bridegroom to lead the bride by the hand ;   he
is accompanied by the best man, and the bride's mother

4. Above—Agamemnon and Briseis
Below—Embassy to Achilles

or the bridegroom's or both take part. In the case of
Paris and Helen Æneas appears as best man, and the two
female figures who join in have the names of Aphrodite
and Peitho. On the Briseis vase, Agamemnon himself leads
her away, accompanied by the herald Talthybius and Diomedes ; the painter has evidently been thinking more of
the result than of the narrative as given in the Iliad ; for

5. Pursuit of Troilus by Achilles

though Agamemnon threatened to come and take Briseis
away, he did not do so in person, but sent his heralds.

A good example of the way in which a traditional
subject or motive is adapted or combined with another is
offered by the tale of Troilus. According to the literary
tradition this ran more or less as follows. He was the

youngest son of Priam, and was sent to water the horses at a fountain. Achilles lay in wait for him and pursued him; and having caught him, slew him by beheading him at the altar of Apollo Thymbræus. His brothers came out too late to rescue him, and a fight took place over his body. Various scenes from this story are represented on Greek vases. These will be noted in their proper place.

6. Death of Troilus

But there is a strange variant. On a black-figured vase Achilles is represented as hurling the boy Troilus by one leg against an altar. Now this motive belongs properly to the representation common on vases of the death of Astyanax after the capture of Troy, when Neoptolemus, the son of Achilles, hurls the boy Astyanax by the leg against an altar – usually the altar at which Priam has taken refuge. This motive is evidently a reminiscence of Andromache's foreboding that " some one of the Achæans should seize him by the arm (not the leg, as in the picture) and hurl him from the tower." The vase is question, however, cannot represent the death of Astyanax, for in the upper part of the picture are to be seen the battlements of Troy still standing, and behind them the Trojan heroes drinking and feasting, in ignorance of the tragedy going on outside. It must therefore be intended to represent the death of Troilus. The resemblance between the two stories must have struck the artist, since in both cases the youngest prince of the family of Priam is ruthlessly

7. Neoptolemus slays Astyanax and Priam

slaughtered, in the one case by Achilles, in the other by his son and successor Neoptolemus. And the " contamination " of the two subjects does not work in one direction only. It is expressly stated in the case of Troilus that Achilles cut off his head, and this is emphasised in some of the pictures ; in some instances the severed head is actually thrown by Achilles at the avenging Trojans. But in a lecythus representing the death of Priam not the corpse but the head only of Astyanax is being hurled against the aged king. In such cases as this it may be difficult to decide whether the two stories were actually confused by the artist, or whether he merely wished to adapt a familiar motive to a new use or meaning.

Often, however, the source of variation in treatment is not so simple and obvious. This is particularly the case when the decorative principle is involved. Sometimes the shape of the space to be decorated dictates the addition of other figures. For example, a group which may be repeated without any individual significance consists of a warrior and a lady who offers him a parting cup. It is often necessary to extend this group by the addition of other figures balancing each other on either side. Then

8. Neoptolemus with the head of Astyanax

these may be given the names of Priam and Hecuba, and the warrior is Hector; or they may be Peleus and Thetis, and the warrior is Achilles.

It would be easy to multiply instances of this process; but it seems better to reserve other examples for their due place in this study.

Before considering the relations of the poet and the artist during various epochs, it is advisable to take a brief survey of the conditions under which the artist and more especially the vase-painter carried out his work. The designs are for the most part drawn in outline, and then, in earlier times, filled in with a black silhouette, and details are added by means of incised lines, often of very fine workmanship ; after about the middle of the sixth century B.C. this method is superseded by another, in which the background is filled in with black, and the figures are left in the natural colour of the terra-cotta, or sometimes in white ; and details are drawn within the outlines in fine and delicate lines.   In the reproductions of vase-paintings given in this book some are given only in outline, others have the outlines or the background filled in with black, thus approximating to the original effect.

The illustrations here reproduced are mostly on a small scale, and their aim is to show the treatment of the subject rather than the style or technique.   They are obviously only a very small proportion of the numerous scenes on Greek vases which might be quoted to show the varying treatment of Greek myths upon vases ; and they have been chosen not so much for their intrinsic interest as for the light they throw upon the methods of selection and representation which appeal to the vase-painter.   In order to appreciate the character and composition of the various scenes, it must be remembered that the decorative element is very strong in most of them.   They were intended for the decoration of vases of various shapes. Sometimes a single scene occupies the whole decorated surface ; sometimes it is broken up by the handles or other divisions into two or more subjects.   These again may either be entirely independent, or may represent subjects which are more or less closely related to one another.   And in any case figures are often added merely to fill the available space or to suggest other persons who, though not likely to be present at the scene, might reasonably be expected to take an interest in it.   Examples of all these will occur in the course of our study.

CHAPTER II

THE ILIAD

WHATEVER opinion may be held as to the exact date of the composition of the Iliad, there can hardly be a doubt that it falls into the period between the early splendour of Cretan and Mycenæan art and the painted vases from which most of our illustrations of Greek literature are derived. Consequently we cannot expect to find pictures of Homeric scenes made by artists who were even approximately contemporary with the subjects they represent. Works of art are rarely described in the Homeric poems; when they are so described, they are usually examples of decorative metal work or engraved gems, such as the brooch of Odysseus, with a dog attacking a fawn, or Agamemnon's breastplate, a present from the King of Sidon, and therefore possibly to be thought of as Phœnician in workmanship. The most notable example of an elaborate work of art is the famous shield of Achilles, which was the work of the Greek god Hephæstus. It is not, of course, to be supposed that the poet had ever seen such a shield as he describes; but he evidently had in his mind a complete design, of which the symmetry and decorative fitness are remarkable. He probably thought of the design as being carried out in a damascening technique such as we see in the inlaid daggers from Mycenæ. Though many scenes and figures in varied action are described, there is no attempt to represent or to illustrate a mythical story, or even an actual event. All the scenes are merely typical events of town and country life, in peace and war. It is instructive to contrast, in this respect, the Hesiodic Shield of Heracles, in which, among other scenes of a more general character, one or two represent various myths, Perseus and the Gorgons and Cæneus and the Centaurs. For the difference in custom marks the change that had taken place between the dates of the two poems. Perhaps the nearest approach to the kind of scene described in the Homeric shield is to be seen in a fragment of a silver vase with repoussé reliefs found at Mycenæ. Here there is a battle going on between both light and heavy-armed troops outside the wall of a city; "and on the wall there stood to guard it their dear wives and infant children, and with these the old men." The artist who made this cup might well have designed such a work as the shield of Achilles. But there is no indication that he had any particular battle in his mind. And if mythical creatures or monsters such as the Harpies, the Sphinx, the Gorgon, and even the Centaurs are mentioned by Homer, there is no reason to suppose that they were imagined by the poet in the form in which they appear in Greek art of the classical age; a possible exception is the Chimæra, if we consider the detailed description of it as " in front a lion, and behind a serpent, and in the midst a goat, and she breathed dread fierceness of blazing fire." But these monsters, when they appear in early decorative art, at a time later than the Iliad, but not far removed from it, are for the most part merely grotesque conceptions borrowed from oriental art, and not necessarily having any relations to the forms with which they were later identified. There is no reason to suppose, for instance, that the Sirens were thought of by Homer in the form of human-headed birds. This is a matter that will have to be considered later in discussing their relation to later literature (see p. 47).

On early vases it was quite common for animals, both possible and impossible, to be mingled with human forms ; without any relation other than decorative existing between the two. But a mythical meaning could sometimes be given to such propositions, as when a human figure and a sphinx suggest the tale of Œdipus. Such examples, however, fit the story of the Odyssey rather than that of the Iliad. We very often find on vases, as on the Homeric shield, scenes from ordinary life rather than from mythology ; and such scenes may very well serve to illustrate the Iliad. Groups in which two or more warriors face one another, or fight over a fallen enemy, are very numerous ; and they can be made to suit any number of combats recorded in the poem. Very often names are added to identify the various combatants, and thus to give interest. But as a rule the typical combat suffices for the artist ; he does not trouble to follow the details of the text which is usually very explicit both as to the weapons used and the nature of the wounds inflicted. In fact, it seems in many cases that the scene is a commonplace one that would fit many Homeric events, and that the names were added as an afterthought. Sometimes scenes depicted on vases do not fit any event in the Homeric poems, and even represent a mode of fighting not customary at the time. Thus two warriors fighting on foot are often accompanied each by a groom riding one horse and leading another. This can only mean that the warriors fought as mounted infantry, riding to the scene of combat and then dismounting. This we know to have been a common custom in the earlier days of historic Greece ; but it was unknown in the time of Homer, whose warriors fought either on foot or from their chariots, but never rode on horseback, which was regarded rather as an acrobatic trick. Often, even where the course of a combat is described in detail by the poet, a generalised representation is preferred by the artist. For example, in the single combat between Hector and Ajax, the heroes first exchange spear thrusts, and then pick up huge stones to hurl at each other. But on a vase, where Hector and Ajax are identified by name, Ajax is thrusting with a spear, and Hector, who is collapsing, has drawn his sword ; but Apollo stands by him, as in the Iliad. The group, in fact, is practically identical

9. Separation of Ajax and Hector

with that used elsewhere for Achilles and Hector. On this occasion, after their single combat, the two champions were separated by the heralds of their respective sides, Talthybius and Idæus. On one vase, the two combatants are being forcibly separated, as in the strife between Ajax and Odysseus for the arms of Achilles (Fig. 34). In the reconciliation scheme on a vase, the name of Phœnix is substituted for that of Idæus – evidently a mere caprice in the artist's memory ; for this particular scene emphasises the story of the exchange of gifts that were later on to prove fatal, since Ajax gave to Hector the baldric by which he was drawn at the chariot of Achilles,

and Hector gave Ajax the sword with which he slew
himself. This example of the saying " the gifts of foes are
no gifts and profit not " was evidently one that took the
popular fancy long before it was adopted by Sophocles in
his Ajax.

There are some other scenes on vases which follow closely
the version given in the Iliad. One of the most characteristic represents the embassy to Achilles, when Phœnix, Ajax,
and Odysseus were sent by the Greek chieftains to try to
persuade Achilles to abate his wrath (Fig. 4 and Fig. 31).

10. Hector and Ajax exchange gifts

The scene occurs repeatedly on vases, usually in the same
form. Achilles is seated in the midst, his head covered by
his cloak, in an attitude of sulky dejection. Odysseus is
just in front of him, and is evidently trying to persuade
him, while on one side stands Ajax, on the other Phœnix,
their names attached. In one case the third envoy is
labelled Diomedes. This is quite inconsistent with the
story in the Iliad ; for Diomedes was not among those
sent, and criticised the policy of sending them. The vase-
painter probably forgot who was the third, and merely
added the name of the first Greek hero that occurred to
him. On one vase, the scene is amplified by the addition

of other figures, a youth and two maidens ; but this is not inconsistent with the Homeric version, which mentions Patroclus and two maidens as present at the scene. But the addition of other figures such as these to complete or balance the group is a common device of the vase-painter, and is often independent of the literary version.

In the most conspicuous of battle scenes, the final combat of Hector and Achilles, we are expressly told that Hector, having lost his spear, drew his sword, and that Achilles slew him by piercing his neck with a spear. In some

11. Achilles and Hector

instances on vases these weapons are shown (Fig. 11) ; but on one vase not only are both warriors armed with spears, but Hector is wounded in the thigh and collapses.

The ransoming of Hector's body, as described in the twenty-fourth book of the Iliad, is as distinctive and dramatic as any scene in Homer ; and here the vase-painter's version, several times repeated, has a fairly close relation to the text. Achilles is represented as reclining on a couch and still at supper, and Priam advances rapidly towards him. The main divergence from the Homeric description is that Priam's attendants bearing the precious ransom follow immediately after Priam, while in the

Iliad Priam leaves the waggon with the ransom outside, and approaches Achilles alone. But how otherwise could the offering of the ransom, which is an essential part of the story, be indicated? A more striking variation is seen in the fact that the body of Hector, still showing its wounds, is lying underneath the couch on which Achilles is feasting. This is quite inconsistent with the consideration shown by Achilles in not letting Priam see the body until it was washed and anointed and given a seemly covering with the garments that Priam himself had brought as part of the ransom. The artist has evidently chosen to emphasise

12. Ransom of Hector, Priam, and Achilles

the touch of brutality which from time to time is shown by Achilles, rather than his actual courtesy at the moment. The whole scene, in fact, tells the story in a quite different way from the poet, though both alike are following a common tradition. Thus it offers an excellent example of the way the medium of expression affects the treatment of the subject.

There is perhaps no passage in the Iliad that impresses the reader more deeply than the parting of Hector and Andromache. But only one vase painting appears to be reminiscent of it, and that doubtfully. It will be remembered that Hector meets his wife and the nurse carrying

Cg

his child ; that he is about to take Astyanax in his arms,
but his nodding crest frightens the child, so he places it on
the ground and takes the boy from the nurse, and after
a further prayer gives him to Andromache. On an amphora which may allude to this scene there is on one side
a single figure of an armed warrior, on the other a lady
with a child in her arms, who stretches out his hands as if to

13. Hector and Andromache

the warrior on the other side. It is obvious that this representation does not correspond at all closely to the Homeric
narrative. No names are added, and the scene may be
merely a variation on the common theme of the departure
of a warrior from his family. The presence of the child
does indeed differentiate it from most similar representations. But there is no attempt to render either the pathos
or the adjuncts of the scene. And, in the absence of
added names, it is possible to regard the scene as merely a
typical parting.

Among vase paintings which illustrate the Iliad in a general way, none are more common than those which represent scenes of combat, not differentiated to correspond to the Homeric descriptions, even when names are added. The usual scheme represents two spearmen facing each other; sometimes a third lies on the ground between them. An instance on a Corinthian vase shows how little in some cases the painter realised the subject;

14. Æneas and Ajax, Hector and Achilles

on one side the warriors are named Achilles and Hector; behind each is a groom riding with a spare horse, and these are labelled respectively Phœnix and Sarpedon. This is a clear instance of a merely mechanical use of Homeric names to add interest to an otherwise commonplace group. For Phœnix, the aged henchman of Achilles, and Sarpedon, an independent king, are most unsuitable for such a rôle. And on the other side of the same vase is a precisely similar group, with the chief combatants labelled Ajax and Æneas, and the grooms named Ajax (probably from some confused notion of the relation of the two Ajaxes) and the non-committal name Hippocles. It is evidently a misconception to see in this last name an allusion to a different cyclic poem in which Hippocles is mentioned. Then under one of the handles is placed in a crouching or running position a figure named Dolon, a vague reminiscence of a different part of the Iliad. The whole vase offers a warning against taking too seriously the names attached to apparently Homeric scenes. On another vase, of Chalcidian origin, there is a scene, not of combat

15. Helen, Paris, Hector, Andromache

but showing persons in conversation. Here is evidently a scene within the walls of Troy. Several of the figures have names attached. In the middle are two groups, Helen and Paris and Hector and Andromache : behind Hector is Kebriones his charioteer, here mounted on one horse and leading another, like the grooms on the Corinthian vase. Here again we see the attempt to add interest to a commonplace subject by the addition of familiar names.

Combat scenes in which the fight takes place over a fallen warrior are so common both in the Iliad and on vases that it is often impossible to identify them ; but sometimes in this case the names are given. On a Rhodian plate in the British Museum the figures are identified by

16. Fight over body of Euphorbus

name as Menelaus and Hector fighting over the body of
Euphorbus. This is really a minor episode in the tale of
Patroclus, and it may seem strange that it should be
selected on this and other monuments rather than the
fight over Patroclus himself or other similar scenes.
Possibly it was because of the interest in Euphorbus caused
by the statement of Pythagoras that he himself had been
Euphorbus in an earlier incarnation, as he proved by
recognising the shield of Euphorbus dedicated in the
Heræum at Argos by Menelaus. For this fight over the
body of Euphorbus is elsewhere in art identified by the
names of the warriors.

A much greater interest attaches to a class of vase

paintings, mostly of much higher artistic quality, which do not refer to particular episodes in the Iliad, but may be described rather as works of heroic genre, since they show how the artists of the sixth and fifth centuries B.C. thought of the Homeric characters. A simple example is to be seen on an early red-figured amphora signed by Euxitheos. This has a single standing figure on each side, a warrior with the name Achilles and a maiden named Briseis. Here there is no allusion to any specific event, but rather to two characters which play leading parts in the Iliad. Other vases show Homeric figures in personal relations. A vase which is signed by Sosias, and possibly painted by Euphronios, shows Achilles binding up a wound in the arm of Patroclus in which the pain of the patient and the intense care of Achilles are admirably presented. Among parting scenes, in addition to that of Hector and Andromache already referred to, there is one showing Hector receiving the parting cup from Hecuba, while Priam stands by in an attitude of apprehension.

It would be easy to multiply examples of correspondence or divergence between the text of the Iliad and the vase-painters' version of the same themes; but the instances given will suffice to show the differences in tradition and purpose which affect the poet and the painter.

CHAPTER III

THE ODYSSEY

THE Odyssey lends itself in some ways more easily than the Iliad to comparison with artistic representations. For example, many of the scenes of combat on the vases would serve to illustrate almost any of the fights described in the Iliad, especially since the artist takes no trouble to assimilate the details of his pictures to those given in the Homeric story. The Odyssey, on the other hand, consists of a series of fantastic adventures such as can at once be recognised, although the artists deal with them almost as freely as those who take their subjects from the Iliad. A mere enumeration of the adventures of Odysseus suggests at once to the mind a series of pictures as to the meaning of which there cannot be any doubt. Andrew Lang indeed points out, in his introduction to Butcher and Lang's translation, that the Odyssey is " a tissue of old märchen " or folk-tales : " These must have existed for an unknown length of time before they gravitated into the cycle of the tale of Troy. The extraordinary artistic skill with which legends and myths, originally unconnected with each other, are woven into the plot of the Odyssey, so that the marvels of strange and barbaric fancy became indispensable parts of an artistic whole, is one of the chief proofs of the unity of authorship of that poem."

The Odyssey consists of two parts, the tale told by

Odysseus to Alcinous, comprising the events from the departure from Troy to the arrival at Calypso's island ; and the narrative of Odysseus' parting from Calypso, his return to his native land, and the destruction of the suitors.   Accordingly in the one, which consists of Books IX. to XII., the story is told in the first person, and in the other, Books I. to VIII. and XIII. to XXIV., the poet himself is narrator, and the tale is in the third person.   Both parts contain many episodes which lend themselves to illustration.   It will be convenient to take them in

17. Odysseus and Cyclops (Aristonous Vase)

accordance with the sequence of events rather than in the order in which they appear in the poem.

The first of these adventures to appeal to the vase-painters was that with the Cyclops Polyphemus.   The incidents which they chose to represent were the devouring of Odysseus' companions by the Cyclops, the offering by Odysseus of the cup of strong wine which overpowered the monster, the preparation and heating of the Cyclops' club, the thrusting of it into his one eye, and the escape of Odysseus and his surviving companions by clinging to the sheep as they passed out of the cave.   Accessories such as the cave itself, and the baskets of cheese stored on poles, also occur. Some of them are separately treated,

some are combined together. On a very early vase signed
by Aristonous there is a spirited composition. The
Cyclops is seated on the ground, and Odysseus and four
companions thrust the stake into his eye ; the last of
them presses his foot against the edge of the picture, as if
to get a better purchase. Behind the Cyclops is a stake
supporting a cheese-basket. The monster is on the same
scale as the Greeks. According to the Odyssey, when

18. Odysseus and Cyclops (Laconian Vase)

those who were to assist Odysseus with the club were
selected by lot, the lot fell upon those four whom Odysseus
himself would have chosen. The number on the vase
corresponds with this ; but this coincidence may be
merely accidental, and may depend more upon the amount
of space available than on any desire to follow the narrative in detail. On an early Laconian (or Cyrenaic) vase
the scene is treated by the comprehensive method ; as
much of the story as possible being included in a single
picture. The companions of Odysseus are in this case

three only. The Cyclops, who is of gigantic stature compared with them, is seated upon a rock. Odysseus, while guiding the club into the Cyclops' eye with one hand, offers with the other a cup of wine, though this must have been done long enough before for the Cyclops to fall into a drunken sleep. The cannibal feast is also represented ; for the Cyclops holds in his hands two human legs, which could indeed remain after he had devoured the rest of the victims, but which evidently are intended to complete the story. And the effect of the red-hot club upon the Cyclops' eye is represented by a huge snake, which symbolises the action of the destructive element. This vase-painting really offers as good an example as can be found of the desire to include all the successive events of a story in a single scene. On another vase, while Odysseus and a companion are blinding the Cyclops, who is recumbent on the ground and of huge size, another companion, at the other end of the picture, is represented as heating a club in a fire. This does not probably mean that the same object, here the club, is represented twice in the same scene, but rather indicates the heating of the club in the fire as part of the tale, very much as when Troilus[1] is pursued by Achilles when he had gone to water the horses, and his errand is suggested by other young Trojans drawing water from the spring.

Another scene from the adventure with the Cyclops is the escape of Odysseus and his companions from the cave, by means of the flock of sheep. This is a very common subject upon black-figured vases. In its simplest form it consists only of one or more sheep with Odysseus and some of his companions hanging beneath them, usually tied on by thongs, Odysseus being distinguished from the others by a beard and a sword ; sometimes he goes first, but in

[1] See p. 64.

other cases the Homeric account is followed according to which he came last on the Cyclops' favourite ram ; in one case this ram has a drooping carriage which suggests the way in which the Cyclops addressed it – " Now thou art the very last. Surely thou art sorrowing for the eye of thy lord, which an evil man blinded." No attempt is made to render the device of tying three sheep together with a man under the middle one, nor of Odysseus clinging only to the wool of the ram. In most of these representations the Cyclops does not appear ; but in some he is represented as seated on the ground at the entrance of his cave, and feeling the sheep as they go out. It is not easy to decide in this case whether the simpler form was the earlier one, to which the Cyclops came later to be added, or whether the more complete version is the earlier type, from which portions were later selected. Both alike appear on earlier and later vases, mostly black-figured ; the simpler form is found on a red-figured example. The adventure with Circe also appears both in simpler (or abbreviated) and fuller form. The two main subjects are the transformation of Odysseus' companions into various kinds of beasts, and their deliverance by Odysseus, who threatens Circe with a sword. The presentation by Hermes to Odysseus of the magic herb " moly," which guards him against the power of Circe, is only found on later monuments. The men changed to beasts are represented by human figures with beasts' heads, as if to suggest the Homeric statement that " so had they the head and voice, the bristles and the shape of swine, but their mind abode even as of old." Sometimes these figures alone are to be seen, more often Circe is among them, holding her magic cup and wand. In some cases she is represented seated at her loom, in accordance with the Homeric tale. The usual representation of the deliverance from Circe's magic shows her either standing or seated, and holding her cup. Odysseus approaches and threatens her with drawn sword. In this scene one or more of the companions are present in their transformed shape of beasts – not always swine, as in Homer.

Upon the advice of Circe, Odysseus proceeded next to visit the land of the dead, in order to consult the shade of the seer Tiresias about his further voyage. This interview is not only found on a fine South Italian vase, but was also represented in the famous fresco of Polygnotus in the Lesche at Delphi. This last was an elaborate composition, and included references to many other myths as to the realm of Hades and its occupants. Many of these are also included in the account in the Odyssey ; but they mostly are merely alluded to rather then narrated ; some such as the sack of Troy and the murder of Agamemnon on his return must be considered later, in connection with other poems of the epic cycle and with lyric and dramatic poetry. The chief scene, the interview with Tiresias, is represented on the vase already mentioned in a manner closely resembling the version given in the Odyssey. Odysseus is represented seated over a pit containing the body of a sacrificed ram, and holding a drawn sword to keep off the other ghosts until Tiresias has given his message ; and at the corner of the pit is the head of Tiresias, with white hair, just emerging from the ground. On each side of Odysseus stands a companion, one of them holding a drawn sword over his back, evidently to keep off the spirits of the dead.

On his return to the island of Circe, Odysseus received from her instructions as to the dangers he should escape or avoid on his further journey. The first of these was the island of the Sirens ; in the Odyssey the advice given by Circe is followed closely ; Odysseus placed wax in the

19. Circe and Odysseus

ears of his companions so that they should not hear the song of the Sirens, while he himself was bound to the mast so that he could not break loose. The scene occurs upon several vases ; in the most complete version the whole ship is represented, the crew rowing vigorously and the steersman signalling to them ; Odysseus himself stands upright with his back to the mast, to which he is bound by cords. The Sirens are represented in the form

20. Odysseus' ship and the Sirens

of human-headed birds. Odysseus strains his head upwards towards the Sirens, two of whom are perched on rocks overhanging the ship ; one of them has her name, Himeropa (or lovely voice) written above her. A third throws herself down from the rock ; her eye is closed as if in death. There seems an allusion here to a tale that the Sirens, if their song failed to attract the sailors, hurled themselves down – an incident probably borrowed from the story of Œdipus and the Sphinx, who perished if her riddle were answered. There is no reason to suppose that the poet of the Odyssey thought of the Sirens in this form. The human-headed bird is common as a decorative form on early Greek vases; it was borrowed from Oriental art, and so far as is known it had no mythical meaning in Greece at this time, though it seems both in Eastern and in later Greek art to be connected with death and the tomb. An ingenious suggestion has been made by Miss Harrison that the appearance of the Sirens in this form was accidental in origin, being due to such a generally

21. Odysseus and the Sirens

decorative figure being juxtaposed on a vase to a ship; and the painter thus found ready to his hand a representation of Odysseus' ship and the Sirens which became canonical in later art. On a lecythus from Eretria there are two Sirens, perched on rocks, one playing a lyre, the other a double flute; the sea is represented by a wash of grey, out of which two dolphins are leaping; yet curiously enough, Odysseus is represented as tied not to the mast but to an Ionic column. The passage of Scylla and Charybdis is one of the most familiar of the events recorded in the Odyssey; but it does not lend itself

readily to representation on vases. This is particularly
the case with the whirlpool of Charybdis. Scylla is indeed
described in some detail by Circe when she gives Odysseus
his sailing directions, and these details are repeated when
he actually passes the strait. " She has six necks exceeding long, and on each a hideous head, and therein three
rows of teeth set thick and close, up to her middle is she
sunk far down in the hollow cave, but forth she holds her
heads from the dreadful gulf, and there she fishes. . . .
Thereby no sailors boast that they have fled scatheless
ever with their ships, for with each head she carries off
a man." And this is just what happens when the ship
of Odysseus passes. The description might well have
tempted the imagination of an artist who enjoyed the
horrible and monstrous ; but the Scylla who is represented
on some vases and other works of art has no resemblance
at all to the Homeric description, but is merely a female
figure to the waist, with a fish-like or snaky tail such as is
found in Triton and other sea-monsters. In fact, the
later conception of Scylla has no clear relation to the
monster described in the Odyssey. Whence the type of
Scylla came it is not easy to decide ; but such fish-
tailed creatures are common in Ionic art and in the archaic
island gems ; hence it was borrowed without any attempt
to identify it with the monster described by Homer.

The further adventures of Odysseus, before he arrived
at Calypso's isle, do not offer much opportunity for
illustration. After his ship was wrecked and all his companions destroyed he was on two occasions reduced to a
raft – after the wreck of his ship to an improvised one
made of the mast and keel of his ship; afterwards, when he
left Calypso, to one carefully constructed with her aid.
An allusion to one of these occasions may be recognised
in a rough caricature on a Bœotian black-figured vase,

showing Odysseus crossing the sea on a rudely constructed raft.

With the arrival of Odysseus at Phaeacia and his meeting with Nausicaa the character of his adventures changes. He no longer wanders among strange monsters, but has to deal with human beings like himself, and his return to his home in Ithaca has nothing miraculous

22. Odysseus and Nausicaa

about it – except perhaps for the voyage from Phaeacia to Ithaca in a single night. Consequently the vase-painter finds subjects that are more full of human interest, but that offer less scope to fantastic imagination. In the scene of the meeting of Odysseus with Nausicaa the vase-painter is evidently inspired by the Homeric narrative; but while he follows it closely in some matters, in others

Dg

may have known of this ; but it is likely enough that the third figure is simply added to complete the scheme.

The tales of the sack of Troy and of the murder of Agamemnon upon his return home are referred to in the Odyssey ; but there were fuller versions of these in the other cyclic poems and in the works of the Attic dramatists, so that it is more convenient to defer their consideration until we come to consider those branches of Greek literature.   On the other hand, the further adventures of

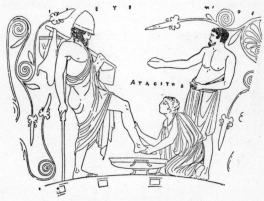

24. Odysseus and Eurycleia

Odysseus after he had reached his home in Ithaca offer only a few, but those very distinctive subjects to the vase-painter.   One of them is the recognition of Odysseus by his old nurse Eurycleia (her name is given as Antiphata on the vase – probably merely by a slip of memory).   The scene is depicted much as in the Odyssey.   The old nurse is washing Odysseus' foot in a large bowl, and touches with her other hand the scar made by the boar upon his leg.   He is represented as a traveller, wearing a pointed cap and carrying a bundle on his shoulder.   The main difference in the picture here is that the faithful swine-herd Eumæus is present and apparently taking notice of what is happening; and that Penelope is absent, though the poet says she was present, but did not observe Eurycleia's recognition of her master.

The culminating scene of the Odyssey is the slaying of the suitors in the palace of Odysseus. This occurs on a vase which in some ways follows closely the story of the Odyssey; it represents the stage of the combat in which Odysseus is still shooting his arrows, and the suitors, as in the poem, are holding up the " tables for shields against the arrows of swift death." But neither party has yet

25. Odysseus slaying the Suitors

received the arms which they subsequently acquired. But the question is here somewhat complicated; for the group on the vase resembles also very closely a relief representing the same subject found at Trysa in Lycia. This resemblance is most remarkable in the attitude of a figure whose back is transfixed by an arrow which he tries to reach with his hand, and who is in a position im-possible to reconcile with the description in the Odyssey, for the suitors there are shot from the front. It is evident that these two compositions are derived from a common original; and it has been suggested that this original must have been one of the great frescoes painted by Polygnotus. It is actually recorded that he painted in poet, either Stasinus or Hegesinus. It began with the capture of Thetis by Peleus, and their wedding, which was attended by all the gods. At this feast Eris (Discord) caused the contest as to beauty between the three goddesses, Hera, Athena, and Aphrodite. Aphrodite, being awarded the prize by Paris, promised him Helen as his wife; and Paris accompanied by Æneas made the expedition to Sparta to persuade her to elope from Menelaus. The Greeks gathered together under Agamemnon to attack Troy. Many incidents portrayed by the vasepainter were included in the Cypria – for instance, the fight between Idas and Lynceus and the Dioscuri, the feigned madness of Ulysses, the fetching of Achilles from Scyros, the sacrifice of Iphigenia, the fight between Achilles and Telephus, the wounding of Philoctetes by a snake. Dr. Monro says, " The whole poem must have been composed as an introduction to the Iliad."

The events described in the Iliad come next in order, containing incidents from the quarrel of Achilles and Agamemnon to the funeral of Hector.

Then comes the *Æthiopis* composed by Arctinus of Miletus. It takes its name from Memnon, the Prince of the Æthiopians, who came to help the Trojans, and was slain by Achilles. The end of the Iliad was immediately followed by the arrival, as a Trojan ally of the Queen of the Amazons, Penthesilea, who also met her death at the hands of Achilles. This poem includes the death of Achilles by Paris's arrow, the fight over his body and arms, the contest between Ajax and Ulysses for the arms, and the consequent suicide of Ajax.

This contest recurs at the beginning of the *Little Iliad* of Lesches, which continues the tale up to the capture of Troy, including the fetching of Neoptolemus the son of Achilles from Scyros and of Philoctetes from Lemnos, the

seizure of the Trojan Palladium by Odysseus and Diomedes, and the making and offering of the Wooden Horse
with the ambushed Greeks inside it. This poem is said to
have been followed by Polygnotus in his famous fresco at
Delphi representing the capture of Troy. Aristotle says
that ten tragedies were founded upon incidents recorded
in the Little Iliad ; and the vase-painters also derived
many subjects from it.

The *Iliupersis* of Arctinus also describes the capture of
Troy ; in this it overlaps the *Little Iliad*, and gives, as we
shall see, a somewhat different version of this event. In
this poem the chief hero is Neoptolemus; it includes the
tale of Laocoön and of the survival and escape of Æneas.
It contains many references to the Iliad, such as the death
of Astyanax by being hurled from the battlements of
Troy. The death of Priam is differently narrated in the
Little Iliad and the *Iliupersis* ; and the treatment of this
subject by the vase-painter differs from both.

The next poem, the *Nostoi*, deals with the adventures of
the different heroes on their return voyage from Troy.
Among these are some referred to in the Odyssey, particularly those which give the subsequent story of the
Atridæ. The treacherous murder of Agamemnon on his
return to Mycenæ and the vengeance of Orestes are most
familiar to us from the Attic drama, which will have to
be considered in a later chapter.

The *Telegony* appears to have been composed to meet
the demand for a sequel to various tales mentioned in the
Iliad and Odyssey, e.g., the subsequent adventures and
death of Odysseus ; but it does not appear to have offered
a suitable field for the vase-painter's imagination.

All these works, though they vary greatly in period and
poetical merit, are essentially epic in their continuous
narrative, and so may be clearly distinguished from the

lyric and dramatic treatment of the same or similar themes
in later Greek poetry.

The relation of the vase-painter to those tales contained
in the Epic Cycle can most easily be realised by a somewhat detailed study of individual examples; and it will
be convenient to consider them more or less in the order
in which they appear in the narrative. Achilles being the
chief hero of the *Cypria*, the capture of Thetis by Peleus
and their wedding festivities are favourite subjects for
representation on vases. In the simplest groups the god-

26. Peleus seizing Thetis

dess is being seized round the waist by the youthful hero.
In the narrative it was doubtless told how she, as a sea-
goddess, changed herself into various shapes in her effort
to escape. The vase-painter finds a means of expressing
the same incidents by representing a snake or a lion or
both attacking Peleus as if in an attempt to free her; on
one vase flames of fire spring from her shoulders. Sometimes this group of two figures fills the whole available
field; in others, various other figures are added to fill the
space or to balance the composition. In some cases there
are Nereids, the sisters of Thetis, or the centaur Chiron;
on a vase painted by Duris the row of astonished Nereids

is continued on the other side of the vase, and one of them rushes up to their father to tell the tale, and throws her arms round his neck. In all these vases Thetis is fully draped.

On a fourth-century Attic vase, from Camirus in Rhodes, the scene is differently imagined, as if it were a surprise of bathers. Thetis, who is in a crouching position, is just disrobing, and is grasped by Peleus by the arm, and a sea monster curls round his leg and bites it, while a flying Eros sets a garland on his head; the group is surrounded by other Nereids (partly dressed or undressed), one of them in flight. Thus, as Dugas says, "the mysterious character of the old myth is almost entirely lost, and all that we have before us is a picture of a lovely bather amid her companions, surprised by a gallant young man, whose boldness is already crowned by love." The drawing is very free and even florid in style; and the figure of Thetis is distinguished by its white pigment, while the other female figures, as well as Peleus, remain in the natural terra-cotta colour of the vase. The whole shows a strong contrast to the severe and simple treatment we find in sixth- and fifth-century representations of the subject.

The marriage feast of Peleus and Thetis is to be seen on the principal frieze of the famous François vase. At one end is the palace of Peleus, represented as a square hall with a porch supported by two columns in front; this faces the spectator, and through the door Thetis can be seen seated within. In front of the palace stands Peleus, beside an altar on which stands a cup. He welcomes the approaching guests. Then comes the procession of the gods, led by Iris and the centaur Chiron, who grasps Peleus by the wrist, and carries over his shoulder a present of game for the wedding feast, to which Dionysus

brings an amphora of wine. The rest follow in a long procession, each of the chief gods in a separate chariot accompanied by his proper consort; they are accompanied by
others on foot, mostly minor deities such as the Fates,
the Muses, and the Seasons. It is to be noticed that
the whole composition does not appear to have been
designed especially for this vase; for the handles are
applied in such a way as not only to interrupt the sequence
of the whole, but also to cover portions of the figures
which should have occupied the concealed space.

The next episode in the tale of Troy offers a favourite
subject to vase-painters and other artists of all periods;
this is the Judgement of Paris. The contest between the
three goddesses, Hera, Athena, and Aphrodite, had arisen
at the marriage feast, and Paris was called on to decide
it. The simplest form of this subject, which is common on
black-figured vases, consists merely of the three goddesses
advancing in procession, led by Hermes – a device common enough in representations of the nymphs or similar
triads. Paris is either absent, or awaits their arrival.
Sometimes he is singing to the lyre, sometimes he seeks to
escape, and is detained by Hermes. In early examples the

27. Judgement of Paris (Hieron)

three goddesses are only slightly differentiated, if at all.
Athena has sometimes a helmet, sometimes the ægis only

as her distinctive attribute. All three are fully draped.
Hermes sometimes merely leads the procession as a herald,
sometimes he seeks to detain Paris, who is running away.
Later on the different figures are more clearly realised ;
Aphrodite is accompanied by one or more Erotes, who
flutter around her. Paris comes to be seated in the
middle, with the goddesses grouped around him, and
Hermes stands by him as if to offer his advice. Later still
the composition and drawing are easier and more florid.
On a South Italian vase the preparations for the contest
are rendered ; Hera holds aside her veil and looks into a
hand-mirror, Aphrodite is having a bracelet clasped on to
her wrist by Eros ; and Athena, who has laid her shield and
helmet aside, is washing her hands and arms in the stream
that flows from a lion-head in a fountain house. Paris, in
this and other later vases, wears an ornate Phrygian cap.
On a vase of very florid style from Kertch in the Crimea,
Eris and Themis are present as spectators in the background ; and the upper corners of the field are occupied by
two chariots, with female charioteers, who may have
brought Eris and Themis as interested in the event. A
curious variation of the procession scheme is found on a
vase of about the middle of the fifth century. Paris is
seated on a rock, with his dog and a sheep, Hermes intro-
duces the goddesses, who approach each in her own
chariot, Hera drawn by four horses, Athena by a pair of
snakes who form part of the chariot itself, and Aphrodite
by a pair of Erotes. The familiar type of the Judgement of
Paris in later Græco-Roman and in modern art, in which
the goddesses cast aside all their garments when they
submit to judgement, is unknown to Greek vase-painting,
which always represents the three rival goddesses as fully
draped. It is to be noted that the apple makes no appearance on these vases. It does not come into the story as

given in literature until the Hellenistic age, when it also
appears on pictures of the subject. In earlier versions
Eris (Strife) causes the contest between the three goddesses, but we are not told exactly how that strife arose.
The expedition of Paris to win the promise of Aphrodite,
the fairest woman on earth, is the subject of many vases,
showing his reception by Helen, and the persuasion of

28. The three Goddesses in their chariots

Aphrodite and sometimes of Eros also. But the most
characteristic is an adaptation of a wedding procession on
the vase by Hieron painted by Makron.[1] Here Paris leads
Helen by the wrist, and Æneas, as in the story, accom-
panies Paris as " best man," while Aphrodite and Peitho
(Persuasion) take the places of the bride and bridegroom's
mothers. The departure of Paris and Helen in a ship may
be the subject of an early geometrical vase now in the

[1] Cf. Fig. 3.

British Museum. Here a man is just embarking and leading a woman on board by the wrist ; but the intention of the artist here may merely be an ordinary scene of departure.

Other subjects earlier than the tale of the Iliad occur on vases, and more on later paintings, for example the wounding and healing of Telephus by Achilles, and the attack by the serpent on Philoctetes. But the favourite subject of the vase-painter in the earlier years of the Trojan expedition was the slaying of Troilus by Achilles. This subject seems to have appealed in a peculiar way to the imagination of the early artist. Troilus was the youngest son of Priam, and his death was accompanied with acts of cruelty such as do occasionally mark the character of Achilles. The story really falls into a succession of events, some of which come to be blended together in what is called the comprehensive method, of which the application to the story of Troilus has already been mentioned in the introductory chapter. The incidents in succession are as follows[1] : First Achilles is represented as crouching in wait behind the fountain towards which Troilus is riding the horses to be watered, sometimes accompanied by his sister Polyxena, who brings a pitcher to be filled at the fountain. Then comes the pursuit scene. Achilles pursues and seizes Troilus, dragging him off his horse, while Polyxena escapes to the city gate. When she brings the news to her father Priam other Trojan heroes sally forth to the rescue. Meanwhile Achilles drags Troilus to the altar of Apollo Thymbræus, and slays him by decapitation – always in Greek feeling a brutal act. Over the headless body a fight takes place beside the altar, more warriors on each side joining in the fray. In one or two cases Achilles actually hurls the

[1] Cf. Figs. 5 and 6.

severed head of Troilus as a missile. Almost every one of these successive incidents of the story is found as a separate representation on vases. On the François vase is a treatment which is quoted by Professor Robert as a typical example of the comprehensive method. The subject occupies a long frieze with numerous figures. In the middle is the chief group – the swift-footed Achilles is on the point of catching Troilus, who gallops away riding one horse and leading another. The scene is defined at one end by the gate of the city of Troy, at the other by the fountain to which he was taking the horses. The space between the central group and the fountain is filled by figures of the gods, Athena, Hermes, and Thetis as favouring Achilles' attempt, and Apollo, who is behind the fountain, is in an attitude of protest, a reminder to the spectator that his altar was to be desecrated ; and near the fountain are another Trojan youth and maidens, indicating that it was the customary watering-place. In front of the city gate Priam is seated, in conversation with Antenor, and towards them runs Polyxena, having dropped her pitcher on the ground, and reports the attack on Troilus. Behind Priam two of Troilus' brothers, Hector and Polites, sally forth to the rescue fully armed. The method adopted in representing this scene is clearly characterised by Professor Robert in his *Bild und Lied*. The painter's art is " seldom content to show only Polyxena, dropping her pitcher in terror, Troilus leaping away on his flying horses, Achilles with mighty strides pursuing him. It enlarges the type and represents the fountain also (omitted on the left of Fig. 5) ; and as if nothing had happened, as if the royal children were in no deadly danger, a Trojan youth is occupied in filling his pitcher, without a glance at the flying Troilus, without betraying any apprehension that his return to the city is cut off and his destruction threatened. The artist wishes to show the activity at the fountain near the city, but he represents it as it usually goes on in quiet days, not as it must have been at the moment when the threat of danger approached the town in war. The same lack of unity in conception meets one at the other end of the scene, where the goal of flight, the town-wall of Troy, is represented. In front of the wall Priam is seated on a stone seat, and Antenor informs him of the danger in which his children are placed : Hector and Polites hasten out of the gate to the help of their threatened brother. It is evident that events are here represented which cannot have taken place at the same time. At the moment when Antenor gives Priam the first news, Hector and Polites might well be arming themselves, but they could not already rush forth from the gate ready for the fray. What we can here comprehend with a single glance was in the poem which gave poetical form to this tale, the *Cypria*, a sequence of events. But it would be a mistake to think the painter has here intended to represent three scenes distinguished in time. Narration by a series of scenes is entirely alien to archaic art. It compresses all together in one scene, but it is a scene without any sharp definition of the moment." It is to be noted that in this comprehensive method of representation the same figure never appears twice in the same scene in consecutive actions ; such a device is common in oriental art and also, as Wickhoff points out, in Roman reliefs such as the column of Trajan. The tale of Troilus is concluded in two separate scenes upon a vase by Euphronius ; one of these shows Troilus being dragged away by Achilles ; in the other Achilles seizes Troilus by the hair, while in his other hand he wields the sword to behead him.

But even this series of separate or combined events

E G

does not exhaust the vase-painter's resources.[1] On a black-figured vase is represented a warrior who swings a boy by the leg and apparently hurls him against an altar. This does not correspond to any literary version of the story of Troilus; but it does at once suggest comparison with another event no less familiar, the death of Astyanax as foretold by Andromache in her famous lament over Hector, how he should be hurled by some Greek from the battlements. This version of the death of Astyanax occurs frequently upon vases representing the sack of Troy, which we shall have to consider separately in their due place. At first sight it may appear that this vase represents the death of Astyanax as mentioned in the Iliad. But this appears impossible, since the battlements of Troy are depicted on the vase, with warriors still carousing upon them. There can be little doubt that we see here an instance of the transference of a type from one story to another; and the transference is the more natural in this case because both victims are slain with unusual cruelty, because both are at the time the youngest scion of the royal house of Troy, and because the slayer is in the one case Achilles, and in the other Neoptolemus, the son of Achilles and his successor as the leading hero among the Greeks.

The ten years which elapsed between the landing of the Greeks at Troy and the opening of the Iliad do not offer many opportunities to the vase-painter. There are indeed certain ordinary instances of camp life which are repeated more than once on black-figured vases, the finest one by Exekias showing two heroes in full armour playing at draughts or dice; in this case the heroes are named Achilles and Ajax; an immense amount of detailed care, almost like jewellers' work, is given to the arms and

[1] Cf. Fig. 7.

cloaks of the heroes; their shields lean against the edges of the panel in which the scene is enclosed. The two heroes call out τέσσαρα τρίς, the numbers of their throws.

On another vase signed by Sosias and possibly painted by Euphronios, Achilles is seen bandaging the arm of Patroclus, which has been pierced by an arrow. The arrow, which evidently has just been extracted, lies on the ground. Here the artist has shown his skill in rendering the anxious and intent expression of Achilles and the pain that is indicated by the tense muscles and averted face of Patroclus. Here too the names are added ; without them there would be nothing to identify more than an ordinary incident of a campaign.

The events recorded in the Iliad are immediately followed by the arrival of the Queen of the Amazons, Penthesilea, to offer her assistance to Priam now that the defence of Troy is weakened by the loss of Hector. Battles between Greeks and Amazons occur very frequently both on black-figured and red-figured vases ; but often there is no reason to connect them with the tale of Troy ; in many cases they refer either to the fight of Heracles against the Amazons, or to the battles of the Athenians under Theseus against the Amazons who invaded Attica. On the other hand the name Penthesilea occurs in typical battle scenes where her opponent is Achilles ; she either fights on horseback or is dismounted. But there is found even in black-figured vases a hint that more is meant than an ordinary combat ; and a sentimental version becomes more and more evident ; according to which Achilles fell in love with Penthesilea after giving her her death-blow, and supported her or carried her out of the fray. A striking example is to be seen in a large circular plate of which the painting fills the whole field. Here Achilles is in the act of stabbing her through the shoulder. But as he does so he meets the gaze of her eyes, and the two exchange a glance of love, though it is too late. The exaggerated expression therein given almost reminds one of the " close up " of a cinematograph film. Such attempts at exaggerated facial expression are very rare in Greek vase-painting, though they become common enough at Pompeii and elsewhere in Hellenistic and Roman times.

The hero who gives his name to the Æthiopis, Memnon, is often represented by vase-painters. He himself

29. Achilles and Memnon. Thetis, Eos, and scales

usually appears in full Greek hoplite armour, sometimes with a white linen breastplate ; but his attendants, on a vase in the British Museum, are of negroid type and armed with clubs and bows. This is doubtless due to a notion of the Ethiopians as negroes which does not seem to belong to early traditions. In battle he is sometimes accompanied by others who wear a dress like that of Scythians or Amazons. But what attracted the vase-painter to the story of Memnon was probably its analogy to events in the Iliad. It was when Hector had killed Patroclus that Achilles was roused to take vengeance upon him ; and in cases where two warriors are engaged in single combat, it seems to be almost fortuitous whether the names given to them are Achilles and Hector or Achilles and Memnon. A peculiar interest is aroused in this case by the fact that both heroes are of divine parentage, but only the children of minor divinities and of mortal fathers, Achilles son of Peleus and Thetis, and

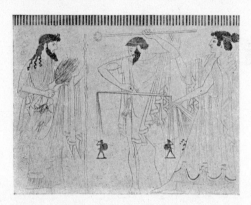

30. Zeus, Hermes, and scales

Memnon of Tithonus and Eos (the Dawn). The two mothers often appear supplicating Zeus on behalf of their respective sons. On a South Italian vase Hermes weighs the fates of the two heroes engaged in combat and the two mothers show gestures appropriate to the issue. There is here a close resemblance to the tale of the death of Hector, when Zeus himself weighed the fates of Hector and Achilles. Another resemblance can be seen between the fates of Sarpedon and Memnon. In both these the divine parent could not save the hero ; but the bodies of both were carried off by special means – for Zeus sent Sleep and Death to carry home Sarpedon, while Eos herself, in a most pathetic vase-painting by Duris, carries off the dead body of her son. When, as in a beautiful vase, in the British Museum, probably painted by Euphronios, the figures of Sleep and Death carry away a dead

31. Above—Embassy to Achilles
Below—Sleep and Death with the body of Sarpedon

warrior, it remains a matter of doubt, in the absence of inscriptions, whether the body is that of Sarpedon or that of Memnon. Sleep and Death are represented as winged figures, one youthful and sometimes one bearded, and the group is repeated on Attic white lecythi to represent the entombment of a mortal.

The death of Achilles by the arrow of Paris, or rather

the fight over his body, is to be seen upon an early Chalcidian vase, which gives a very full representation of the subject. Achilles lies on the ground, his vulnerable

32. Eos with the body of Memnon

ankle pierced by Paris' arrow; another arrow has struck him in the chest. One of the Trojan heroes, Glaucus, has placed a thong round the ankle of the corpse, and strives to haul away the body, but is wounded in the act. Behind him Paris draws his bow with another arrow as he retreats, and Æneas and other Trojans advance to the rescue. Over the body of Achilles, Ajax rushes forward impetuously, and behind him stands Athena, the snakes on her ægis curling around her. At the end of the picture is Diomedes, who has withdrawn for the moment to have a wounded finger bound up by Sthenelos. The whole, in spite of its uncouth drawing, is a most spirited picture of a fight ; and it probably follows quite closely the version of the incident given by Arctinus in the *Æthiopis*, a work which appears in other respects to have been a fairly close imitation of the Iliad.

The vase-painter in this scene seems to have followed a tradition according to which the main credit of rescuing

33. Fight over the body of Achilles

the body and arms of Achilles was given to Ajax. In another version it was said that Ajax carried the body out of the fight while Odysseus kept off the attacking Trojans, and this was the cause of the dispute between the two heroes. It is also alluded to in the panels on the handles of the François vase, where Ajax carries on his shoulder the nude body of Achilles – a detail inconsistent with the recovery of Achilles' arms, and the consequent dispute as to their possession.

This dispute formed a favourite subject both in literature and in art. Ajax and Odysseus each claimed to have been mainly instrumental in rescuing the body and armour of Achilles from the Trojans, Ajax because he actually carried the corpse of Achilles out of the fray, Odysseus because he made this rescue possible by holding off the attacking Trojans. There are different versions of the means by which a decision of the dispute was made ; but all alike agree that the arms were awarded to Odysseus, and that Ajax, driven mad by jealousy, fell upon his sword. Successive scenes in the dispute may be

34. Ajax and Odysseus dispute over arms of Achilles

seen on a vase painted by Duris. In the first the two disputants, Ajax and Odysseus, are being held back by Agamemnon, Phœnix, and others. Ajax has already put on the breastplate, but has not yet fastened one of the shoulder straps. He has drawn his sword, and advances impetuously. Odysseus has as yet only half drawn his sword from its scabbard. The whole group is full of life and vigour, and has often been imitated, notably in Meissonnier's well-known picture. The arms of Achilles lie on the ground between the combatants. The next scene (on the other side of the vase) shows how the decision is made. In the middle is a low pedestal or altar, behind which stands Athena as presiding judge. The Greek warriors approach it from either side to record their votes by placing a pebble on the altar. The decision is not doubtful, for the pile of pebbles on the side of Odysseus is obviously much larger than that contributed by the supporters of Ajax. The expression of the two is characteristic ; Ajax stands in an attitude of dejection, his head averted and muffled in his cloak ; and Odysseus raises his two hands and looks on with a somewhat exaggerated indication of pleasure and surprise. A sequel is given in the interior subject of the same vase, when Odysseus is seen handing on the arms, shield, breastplate, helmet and greaves, to a youth who can hardly be any but the due inheritor, Neoptolemos, the son of Achilles. This dispute for the arms was a prominent incident in both the *Æthiopis* of Arctinus and the *Little Iliad* of Lesches, but we have no means of judging which, if either, more closely corresponds to the Duris vase. The representation of Ajax falling upon his sword occurs on early vases. According to tradition this was the very sword which Hector gave to him in exchange for the baldric by which Achilles dragged the corpse of Hector at his chariot-wheels.

Various events, as to which we have more or less literary record, took place between the suicide of Ajax and the capture of Troy. The Palladium, or sacred image of Athena in her temple on the acropolis of Troy was regarded as the guardian of the city, which could not therefore be captured so long as this Palladium was preserved. An attempt to carry it off was therefore required, and such an attempt was successfully made by Odysseus and Diomedes. Their respective shares in the exploit was variously recorded ; and became the subject of a dispute which reminds us of the similar quarrel between Odysseus and Ajax over the arms of Achilles. This resemblance struck the Attic vase-painters so vividly that they used the same type and composition for both. On a vase signed by Hieron as potter (and painted probably by Makron) the composition is almost identical with that on the Duris vase just described. At one end is placed Odysseus, at the other Diomedes ; both have drawn their swords and are held back by the intervening heroes, Agamemnon in the middle with Phœnix, and the Attic heroes, Acamas and Demophon, next to the would-be combatants. The distinctive feature of the scene is that

35. Odysseus and Diomedes with rival Palladia

Odysseus and Diomedes each hold a small image of Athena, with helmet, aegis, and spear. The two images are not identical, but one has the right arm with spear raised above the shoulder, the other holds it at waist level ; both have the ægis on the extended left arm. This duplication has led to much discussion. In the literary version the two heroes dispute as to which is entitled to the credit of carrying off the Palladium ; how they should have one each, as on the vase, is difficult to understand. It is however recorded that several Greek cities claimed to possess the original Palladium which was carried off from

Troy; and it may be that the vase-painter, knowing this claim, wished to indicate the doubt by representing two Palladia in the hands of the two heroes.

The actual capture of Troy provided many subjects for the vase-painter as well as for the painter of great frescoes. The scenes on the vases are many of them dealt with as separate incidents, though these are in many cases combined into extensive compositions. Among the incidents are the death of Priam by the hands of Neoptolemos; the death of Astyanax, son of Hector, who is hurled from the battlements of Troy by Neoptolemos; the Trojan women taking refuge at the image of Athena;

36. Iliupersis (Vivenzio vase)

Ajax Oileus dragging Cassandra from the same image; Menelaus pursuing Helen, who is saved by the intervention of Aphrodite; Acamas and Demophon recovering their mother Æthra, who had accompanied Helen from Sparta to Troy; the escape of Æneas, carrying off his aged father and his household gods. Most of these subjects were included in the *Little Iliad* and the *Iliupersis* – but there seems to have been no very exact correspondence between either of these accounts and the versions followed by the vase-painters. The two compositions most convenient for our purpose are those on a cup by Brygos and on the so-called Vivenzio vase, now generally attributed to Cleophrades. Neither of these adopts the continuous method of narration, although they must deal with

consecutive events. Both alike have a central group
representing the death of Priam and Astyanax; in the
one case Neoptolemos hurls the body of Astyanax by
one leg either against Priam or against the altar on which
Priam is sitting;[1] in the other the body of the child lies
upon Priam's knees, and Neoptolemos brandishes his
sword over Priam's head. In another version, on an Attic
lecythos, Neoptolemos hurls the head only of Astyanax
at Priam.[2] This is a detail which, as has already been
noticed, is transferred by the painter from the story of
Troilus to that of Astyanax, while the other, the hurling
by the leg, is similarly transferred from Astyanax to Troilus.

As to the end of Priam there were two different literary
versions. In the *Little Iliad* of Lesches, Priam was slain
at the altar of Zeus Herkeios in his own palace; in the
Iliupersis of Arctinus he was dragged from the altar, and
slain at the door of the palace. In neither does there seem
to have been any close connection between the death of
Priam and Astyanax; the hurling of the latter from the
battlements was not a thing to be represented easily upon
a vase, and so he seems to be represented as dashed either
against the altar or against Priam. The altar in this case
is probably meant for the altar in Priam's palace; but
beside it, on the two vases just mentioned, are a palm tree
and a tripod, which do not seem appropriate to the altar
of Zeus Herkeios. On the other hand both palm tree
and tripod occur appropriately beside the altar on the
vase with the slaying of Troilus, which, according to
tradition, was the altar of the Thymbræan Apollo, but
are here transferred to the scene in the sack of Troy.

An interesting problem in the interpretation of vase-
painting is here offered. Did the painter intend to represent, by what has been called the comprehensive method,

[1] Fig. 7.   [2] Fig. 8.

inscriptions it is not possible to identify all these figures, but the main purpose of the scene is clear enough.

In the case of this vase, a hydria, the composition is in a single complete frieze. On another vase, a cup signed by Brygos, there are two distinct scenes, and therefore the same figure can appear more than once. On one side is a furious combat between Greeks and Trojans ; at the end is a woman wielding a weapon like the pestle on the Vivenzio vase ; she is trying to protect the flight of a youth behind her. These two figures must be meant for Andromache and Astyanax. They therefore represent an earlier stage in the story. A sequel may be seen on the other side of the vase, where Astyanax's body is being hurled against the altar and Priam. At the other end of this scene a woman is being led away, apparently not unwillingly, by a warrior. Here, without names added, it is difficult to identify the figures. They may be Menelaus and Helen ; the absence of violence is against their being Ajax and Cassandra ; possibly they are Æthra and either Acamas or Demophon, one warrior being enough to complete the composition this side.

Many other vase-paintings might be quoted which show the various incidents of the sack of Troy either separately or in various combinations. The tradition they represented led up to the great fresco of Polygnotus in the Lesche of the Cnidians at Delphi, as described in detail by Pausanias. This, however, showed much more freedom in the identification and action of the figures.

CHAPTER V

HESIOD AND THE HOMERIC HYMNS

ARLY poems other than those included in the Homeric cycle contain many passages either of narrative or of description which may be compared with the versions of the same incidents represented by vase-painters ; and these have the advantage in some cases of being almost contemporary with the literary version. Examples may be found most easily in the (so called) Homeric Hymns, some of which are narrative poems of considerable length and variety. In the Hymn to Hermes the story of the infant god's raiding of the cattle of Apollo is given with some detail – how he slipped from his cradle, drove away and hid the cattle, dragging them backwards and fitting them with improvised sandals, and then slipped back into the cradle and played injured innocence when Apollo came and charged him with the theft. All this is admirably told or indicated upon a red-figured vase. In the corner of the scene is the infant Hermes in his cradle (called by the poet the sacred winnowing fan, from its slipper-like shape). On his head is the petasos or soft hat which is characteristic of the god ; it seems strangely out of place in the cradle, but is doubtless put in to recall the cattle-raiding expedition. Apollo stands beside the infant and is evidently upbraiding him, and the whole of the background is filled up with the cattle, who also appear on the other side of the vase. This is inconsistent with

the story that Hermes had hidden them, and that Apollo
came to make Hermes tell where they were.   But their
presence on the vase is fully in accordance with the vase-
painter's desire to show as much of the tale as possible in
a single scene.   They stand in a confused cluster, as if to
suggest the difficulty in tracking them.

The same subject is treated in a simpler and earlier form
in an Ionic black-figured vase.   Here the baby is represented as lying flat on its back in a cradle supported on
high legs ; and three figures are engaged in a lively discussion over it.   These may be meant for Apollo and

37. Infant Hermes and Cattle of Apollo

Maia, and the bearded figure may be the old man who
directed Apollo in his search.   But in this case no cattle
are present ; and on the other half of the same scene they
are represented as hidden in a cave or bower, out of sight
of the other figures – a version in some ways nearer to the
literary story.

Another " Homeric " Hymn that offers an opportunity
for pictorial imagination is that to Dionysus.   This tells
how the god was carried off as a captive by Tyrrhenian
pirates.   But his bonds were burst, and " then straight-
way a wonder came upon them.   First of all about the

swift black ship sweet wine bubbled forth with pleasant scent and ambrosian odour arose ; and the sailors wondered when they saw. And at once on the top of the mast there stretched a vine on this side and on that, and many clusters of grapes hung from it. And dark ivy wound round the mast with clustered flowers, and graceful fruit arose and all the branches were garlanded." Then the god changed first to a lion and then to a bear, " and the sailors fled in fear to the stern, and to escape an evil fate they all jumped overboard when they saw it into the sea, and changed into Dolphins." There is a black-figured vase signed by Exekias, on which the whole of the inner picture is taken up by a ship with sail set ; a large figure of Dionysus reclining, with a drinking-horn over his shoulder, occupies the whole deck. A vine with branches and clusters of grapes springs from the mast and fills the upper part of the background, while in the lower part seven dolphins seem to sport about the ship. Apart from the story given in the Hymn to Dionysus, one might well suppose that these dolphins were merely intended to typify the sea over which Dionysus is sailing. But there can be little doubt that the vase-painter is thinking of the transformation of the pirates to dolphins. And this interpretation is confirmed by the fact that in the relief on the monument of Lysicrates, some two centuries later, this transformation is actually represented, just as it is in the beast-headed companions of Odysseus in the palace of Circe.

The myth of the making of Pandora is referred to in two passages in Hesiod, once in the *Theogony* and once in the *Works and Days*. The story evidently contains earlier elements. But as given by Hesiod it attracted the imagination of the vase-painter. To punish Prometheus for stealing fire from heaven and giving it to mortals, " Zeus bade Hephæstus to knead clay with water and to mould a beautiful figure of a maiden, like the immortal gods to look upon, and in it to set the voice and strength of a man." And he bade Athena to teach her the craft of weaving a varied web, and golden Aphrodite to pour upon her head grace and love ; and he ordered Hermes the messenger to set in her a shameless mind and a deceitful heart. And the gods obeyed, and decked her with ornaments ; and she was named Pandora, because all the gods made gifts to her. And Zeus sent Hermes to bear her as a gift to Epimetheus, who accepted her in spite of the warning of Prometheus. The subject of the fashioning and decking of Pandora occurs on a fine white-ground bowl in the British Museum, she stands rigidly in the midst, as if fashioned already but not yet endowed with the breath of life ; and beside her stands on one side Hephæstus placing a wreath upon her head, on the other Athena who drapes a cloak on her shoulders. The names of Athena and Hephæstus are added ; but the central figure is named not Pandora but Anesidora – a name otherwise unknown, but probably transferred by the vase-painter from a scene of the arising of the earth goddess, the sender up of gifts (anesidora). On another vase in the British Museum is a similar scene with several other gods present.

A different kind of illustration to Hesiod's *Works and Days* may be seen on a vase of Nicosthenes, which represents ploughmen and sowers, and in which the various parts of the plough as described by Hesiod can easily be identified.

CHAPTER VI

THE LYRIC POETS

THE reputation of Stesichorus and his influence upon his contemporaries and successors appears to have been out of all proportion to the scanty remains of his poems that have survived. Professor Gilbert Murray says, "There was scarcely a poet then living who was not influenced by Stesichorus; scarcely a painter or potter who did not, consciously or unconsciously, represent his version of the great sagas." Unfortunately it is difficult to illustrate this statement in detail, for the very reason that so little is left of his works. But, as Professor Murray remarks, " in tracing the development of any myth, research almost always finds in Stesichorus the main bridge between the earliest remains of the story and the form it has in tragedy or in the late epos." The most obvious case is the tale of the murder of Agamemnon on his return from Troy by Clytæmnestra and Ægisthus and the subsequent vengeance of Orestes. This tale is told three times, with slight variations, in the Odyssey – once by Nestor to Telemachus (III. 302–312); once by Proteus to Menelaus, who repeats it to Telemachus (IV. 532); and once by the shade of Agamemnon to Odysseus in the Nekyia (XI. 410). Nestor dwells rather on the ambition of Ægisthus, and regards Clytæmnestra as more or less the victim of fate; he also tells of the vengeance of Orestes. In Menelaus' account the preparations of Ægisthus are emphasised, his placing of a sentinel to watch for Agamemnon's return, and the slaying of Agamemnon at a banquet to which he was invited, and which seems to have ended in a general mêlée, since Ægisthus' men as well as Agamemnon's were all killed. In the description of the murder given by the shade of Agamemnon himself, its perpetration at a banquet is again described, and it is, above all, the treachery and cruelty of Clytæmnestra that are emphasised ; Agamemnon says he also heard the piteous death-cry of Cassandra.

This is the epic version of the story ; in it there is no trace of some of the incidents which have become familiar to us through the Attic drama and other subsequent works. Among these are the sacrifice of Iphigenia, which later was regarded as the chief motive or at least a contributory motive for the vengeance of Clytæmnestra, the prominent part taken by Electra, the dream of Clytæmnestra which led to her propitiatory sacrifice, and the pursuit of Orestes by the Furies. There is no reference to the axe with which Clytæmnestra had slain Agamemnon, and with which later she attempted to rescue Ægisthus, nor to the deed being done in the bath-chamber, as Agamemnon was struggling into a sewn-up garment. These and other details, not in the epic story, had evidently become part of the accepted version before it was put into its later form by the great Attic dramatists ; they are partly preserved for us by representations on Attic vases and on other works of art which go back at least in type to a time before the middle of the fifth century B.C. ; partly by quotations from or memories of the works of Stesichorus, whose influence on the form of the story may be judged from the Attic drama. In his version Clytæmnestra slew Agamemnon with an axe. The young Orestes was rescued by his old nurse and handed over to the faithful Talthybius, who fled with him to Phocis. Ten

years later Clytæmnestra had a terrible dream of a
dragon with a bloody head, who changes to Agamemnon ; then she bears a dragon who draws blood with
her milk. She sends Electra with offering to Agamemnon's tomb, the nurse accompanying her. As she sits
at the tomb, Orestes, who had been urged by Apollo
to take vengeance on his mother, and Talthybius arrive.
The nurse and Talthybius recognise each other, and then
the brother and sister. Orestes draws his sword and
devotes it to vengeance. He breaks into the chamber
and slays Ægisthus on Agamemnon's throne – Clytæmnestra comes to help Ægisthus, wielding the same axe
with which she slew Agamemnon. Talthybius holds her
back, and then Clytæmnestra is killed. Orestes was
pursued by the Furies, and kept them off with the help of
a bow given him by Apollo.

Many of these motives or incidents are to be found in
the plays written on the subject by the three great tragic
dramatists. The sacrifice of Iphigenia is mentioned by
Pindar, who is in doubt whether it was vengeance against
Agamemnon for this act or her guilty love for Ægisthus
which led Clytæmnestra to the murder of Agamemnon.

The axe is seen in the hands of Clytæmnestra on vases,
both when she is approaching to murder Agamemnon
and when she attacks Orestes to defend Ægisthus.[1]
And many of these details are found upon vases which are
of an earlier date than the great Æschylean trilogy of the
Oresteia, or other plays of the Attic dramatists upon the
same subject. It follows that many details of the story
were already accepted by tradition at this earlier date.
And since these imply a familiar literary version, it is
generally agreed that this version must be derived from
Stesichorus. Consequently, if the works of Stesichorus

[1] Cf. Fig. 50.

were preserved, we should probably find in them many passages which would lend themselves to comparison with the vase-pictures portraying the same events, especially in the poem called the Oresteia.

Stesichorus has in some cases preserved myths or versions of myths otherwise unknown in literature, but represented upon vases. As an example may be quoted the story of how Heracles crossed the ocean to the western land whence he had to fetch the cattle of Geryon, by the loan of the golden cup in which the sun made his journey

38. Heracles threatens the Sun-god

from day to day. This subject is found on several vases in which Heracles, with bow and club, threatens the sun god as he rises out of the sea in his chariot. A later phase of the story is shown in the inside of a bowl, in which Heracles is seen sitting in the cup as it floats across the sea, indicated by wavy lines and fishes and other marine animals.

Many other lyric poems contain passages of narrative or description which may be compared with the treatment of the same subjects by the vase-painter. One of the most striking of these is Simonides' description of Danae with the infant Perseus in the chest in which they had been set afloat. " When in the dædal chest the breath of the wind carried her on and the swaying sea, then great fear came upon her and her cheeks were wet, and about Perseus she threw her arms and said ' O my child, how great is my sorrow ; and thou sleepest in tender forgetfulness in the comfortless bronze-bolted box, in the dark night, and carest not for the salt spray of passing waves upon thy deep locks, lying in thy purple shawl, thy face pressed to mine. If thou knewest what terror was, thou wouldst have bent thy little ear to my words. But I bid thee,

39. Danae in the Tower

sleep, my child, let the sea sleep, and let my trouble sleep.' And may there be some change, O Father Zeus, from thee. But if I utter too bold a word beyond what is right, forgive me."

We do not know how the rest of the story was told by Simonides, though the pathos of this passage gives him a high rank among lyric poets. The vase-painter has no such resources at his disposal, but he tells what he can within his limited means. On a well-known vase illustrating the story of Danae, he has represented on one side Danae seated on her couch in her subterranean chamber, while the shower of gold descends upon her. The other side shows the story of the chest ; an earlier moment is chosen than that described by the poet. The chest, richly ornamented with stars and other devices, occupies the middle of the picture. Danae appears to stand behind it ; it is possible she is meant to be standing in it, but in that case there would be no room for her legs. She holds the child close to her breast. He is represented, as is usual with children in fifth-century art, not as a baby, but as a slender youth, and he holds a ball in his hand. On one side of the chest is King Acrisius, evidently giving orders as to the disposal of the chest ; on the other side of it is

40. Danae in the Chest

a carpenter boring holes in its rim with a bow drill ; his axe is on the ground beside him. The lid of the chest is open, and is doubtless to be fastened down by means of the holes. The artist has evidently intended to give a clear and intelligible version of the well-known tale, without any attempt at pathos or poetical feelings such as are expressed in the lyric of Simonides.

Bacchylides, whose poems have recently been recovered from an Egyptian papyrus, offers perhaps more opportunities than any other lyric poet for a comparison between the literary and the artistic treatment of the same themes. He gives a vivid description of various scenes, and the pictorial imagination which he displays seems almost to bring them before our eyes. The most striking illustration of this quality is to be found in the description of the visit of Theseus to the abode of his father Poseidon. When Theseus was one of the band of Athenian youths and maidens who had to be sent annually to Minos in Crete to be sacrificed to the Minotaur, Minos laid hands on one of the maidens, and Theseus remonstrated, saying that they must suffer their fate, but not outrage as well; Minos appealed to Zeus for a sign, and bade Theseus, if he too was son of a god, to bring back from the depths the ring which Minos cast into the sea. The rest of the tale must be quoted in full. Theseus accepted the challenge, and " his heart was not turned back, but standing on the well-fitted deck he dived, and the brine of the sea received him with welcome. And the heart of the son of Zeus was melted within him, and he bade keep the richly painted ship before the winds, but fate provided another way. And the ship went quickly forward, and the blast of Boreas blew strong behind it. And all the band of Athenian youths trembled when the hero leapt into the sea and the tears poured over their pale cheeks as they thought on their heavy fate.

"But the dolphins that dwelt in the sea bore the great Theseus swiftly to the house of his father, lord of horses, and he came to the abode of the gods. There he feared when he saw the famous daughters of rich Nereus. For from their bright limbs there shone a light as of fire, and about their hair the gold-inwoven bands were tossed, and they delighted their hearts with nimble feet. And he saw his father's consort, the dear and holy ox-eyed Amphitrite in her lovely home ; and she cast about him a purple robe, and set upon his thick locks a beautiful garland, which at her marriage the crafty Aphrodite gave her, woven with

roses. Naught that the gods will is incredible to men of
sense. He appeared beside the light-sterned ship ; he
checked in his imagination the Cnossian leader, when he
came unwetted from the sea, a wonder to all ; and on his
limbs there glittered the gifts of the gods. And the fair-
throned maidens shouted with new rejoicing, and the sea
re-echoed ; and the young men around sang a pæan of
lovely sound."

Several representations of this story are to be found on
vases, mostly of the early fifth century, and so approximately contemporary with the poem of Bacchylides. It
was also the subject of a wall painting by Micon in the
Theseum, which however must be later than most of the
vase-paintings. In the simplest form of the scene Poseidon,
either seated upon a throne or standing, clasps the hand
of Theseus ; and beside them stands Amphitrite holding
a wreath ; so far the group is hardly differentiated from
the common type of scenes of parting or greeting between
father and son. The figures are not set in any surroundings
suggestive of the sea. There are, however, other vase-
paintings which do this. One is the very beautiful bowl
signed by Euphronius, in which Theseus is presented by
Athena to Amphitrite (Fig. 42). A diminutive Triton
supports his feet, and dolphins play around. Her hand and
his are outstretched as if to meet, but no object seems to
pass between them. Poseidon is not present ; but the
painter does not forget that Theseus' exploit is due to the
favour of Athena, who appears here as the patron of the
hero. A fuller development of the same subject is to be
seen on a vase of about the middle of the fifth century, and
therefore later than Bacchylides, and probably influenced
by the painting of Micon in the Theseum (Fig. 41). The
centre of the picture is occupied by Poseidon, reclining on
a couch. Seated above him is Amphitrite, who holds out a

41. Theseus under the Sea

wreath. Theseus stretches his arms towards her, as if to receive it. He is not merely supported by the feet, as in the vase just mentioned, but is actually held up in the arms of a Triton, who is draped in a richly embroidered cloak, beneath which emerges his fish-like tail. Behind Poseidon, but at a higher level, is a group of Nereids, such as is described by Bacchylides. But while the general contents of

42. Theseus and Amphitrite

the picture recall the story as given by Bacchylides, it does not, like a modern illustration, correspond in all details to the description. In particular, the ring thrown into the sea by Minos is not represented, but only a wreath or garland. The wreath is indeed mentioned by Bacchylides, as well as the purple robe given by Amphitrite to Theseus ; but poet and painter alike seem to have forgotten that the recovery of the ring from the sea was to be the test of Theseus' claim to divine parentage. Both seem more taken up with the beauty of the picture called up by their respective imaginations than with the exact details of the narrative ; and this would seem to imply that the tradition of the tale was transmitted by artistic rather than literary tradition.

A remarkable instance of the way in which history, after a quite short interval of time, can develop into myth is offered by the tale of Crœsus as given by Bacchylides in an ode composed only about eighty years after the event

43. Crœsus on the Pyre

which it describes. A yet earlier version is to be seen on the well-known vase showing Crœsus seated on a pyre of wooden logs, on an elaborate throne. In one hand he holds a sceptre, in the other a bowl from which he pours a libation. In front of him an attendant applies two torches to the pyre, which appears to be already blazing throughout, an inconsistency in time that is quite in accordance with the practice of Greek vase-painters. This has led some commentators to say that the two torches are not torches at all, but fans or sprinklers of lustral water. But similar torches are being applied in just the same way to the pyre of Alcmena on the vase by Assteas, reproduced in the *Hellenic Journal*, XI., Pl. vi., and a similar torch, evidently meant to be flaming, is held by a Trojan warrior in the attack on the Greek ships (Baumeister, p. 729). The story of the pyre of Crœsus is given by Herodotus ; but the version in Bacchylides is earlier (the ode was composed 468 B.C.). It is therefore instructive to quote it first.

" Since the ruler of Lydia, Crœsus, when in accord with the fated ordinance of Zeus, Sardis was captured by the army of the Persians, was guarded by Apollo of the golden sword. For he, when the unlooked for day came upon him, would not await the misery of servitude. But he made himself a pyre before his brazen-walled palace, whereon he mounted with his faithful wife and his fair-haired daughters mourning. And raising his hands to heaven he cried, ' Oh mighty fate, where is the gratitude of the gods ? And where is the lord, the son of Leto ? . . . In shameful way are women led away from their well-built halls, and what before was hateful now is dear. It is sweetest to die.' Thus he spoke, and bade his attendant to light the wooden pile. And the maidens cried out and cast their arms about their mother ; for death foreseen is most hateful to mortals. But when the bright force of the terrible fire blazed up, Zeus sent a dark mass of cloud to extinguish the red flame. Naught is incredible that is done by the care of the gods. Then Apollo born in Delos bore away the old man with his slender-limbed daughters to the Hyperboreans and placed them there for his piety, because he sent to holy Pytho the greatest gifts of all mortals."

The version of the story given by Herodotus some twenty years later differs in several important respects. According to this version, Crœsus was taken prisoner and brought to Cyrus, who had a huge pyre constructed and placed on it Crœsus in chains, with fourteen Lydians. Crœsus, remembering the warning of Solon that no man should be counted happy while alive, called out the name of Solon thrice. Cyrus made enquiries and then relented, and ordered the fire which had already been lighted, to be put out. When the flames could not be mastered, Crœsus called with a loud voice on Apollo and prayed him, if he had ever received at his hands any acceptable gift, to come to his aid. Thereupon the sky, which had till then been clear, became covered with a dark cloud, and a storm burst with such violent rain that the flames were speedily extinguished.

When we turn from these two literary versions to the vase, we find an independent representation of the essential fact that Crœsus was placed upon a wooden pyre, which was set on fire. On the other hand, neither the wife and daughters of Crœsus nor the fourteen Lydians are introduced or even hinted at; nor is there any attempt to suggest the rain-storm that put out the fire. Such a thing is not easy to represent on a vase of this period, though in a later stage of art, which may preserve the tradition of the type, the painter Assteas actually represented the storm and the Hyades pouring water from above on the pyre of Alcmena. The quiet and stately figure of the king, richly clad and enthroned and pouring a libation, certainly suggests a voluntary sacrifice; there is no hint of fetters or restraint. Here the vase is much nearer in spirit to Bacchylides than to Herodotus; but it seems to embody a mythical tradition much earlier than either of the literary versions, and only about fifty

Gg

years removed from the historical fact on which it is based.

Another historical king who attracted the attention of the vase-painter was Arcesilas of Cyrene. But the painter in this case does not represent any striking event in the king's career, but rather an ordinary incident of his daily life. He is seen seated on a throne, wearing a sun-hat, holding a sceptre, and with long hair floating down his back. Over his head a sail is stretched as an awning. The scene takes place on board a ship, and from its yard hangs a large pair of scales, on which several men are employed in weighing some woolly substance, probably the Silphium which was the staple article of Cyrenaic commerce. Other men are packing it in sacks and transporting it through a hatch into a store below, evidently the hold of the ship. Under the throne a tame leopard is lying ; and a monkey, a lizard, and birds add to the local colour. There can be no doubt that the scene is laid at Cyrene or its port ; and the class of vase on which it is painted has, mainly on the evidence of this vase, been identified as Cyrenaic. But excavations at Sparta have shown that the style was originated and developed in that town. This does not however preclude the possibility that the Arcesilas vase and others with Cyrenaic subjects may have been pro- duced by a local variety of this Spartan fabric, just as the Naucratis pottery shows a local development of the style of Miletus, or that of Daphnæ of the style of Clazomenæ.

The Arcesilas vase does not indeed, like that with Crœsus, directly offer comparison with a literary version of the same subject. But the wealth and prosperity of the princely family of Cyrene are celebrated in various passages of Pindar's odes, and therefore it was not unnatural for the vase-painter to represent the source of this wealth and the commercial activity of the dynasty.

Bacchylides seems to have been especially attracted by the Attic legends that afforded subjects for the vase-painter, particularly those concerning the hero Theseus, who seems to have been extolled in rivalry with the Doric Heracles. Sometimes, as on the Treasury of the Athenians at Delphi and on the Theseum at Athens, the exploits of the two heroes are represented side by side. More often the exploits of Theseus form a separate series, which became almost as canonical as the famous twelve labours of Heracles. Bacchylides' description of Theseus' visit to the palace of Poseidon beneath the sea to fetch Minos' ring has already been quoted. His earlier adventures on his journey from Trœzen to Athens by land are mentioned by Bacchylides in a " dramatic lyric " giving a conversation between Ægeus and Medea. The latter expresses her apprehensions as to the reported approach of a formidable stranger, and Ægeus answers her as follows :

" The herald has just come on foot by the long way of the Isthmus, and he tells unheard of exploits of a mighty man. He has slain the violent Sinis, who was strongest of men, the son of the Lytæan son of Kronos, the earth-shaker ; He has killed the man-slaying sow in the groves of Krommyon, and the arrogant Skiron, And he has stayed the wrestling of Kerkyon, And Prokoptas has dropped the strong mallet of Polypemon, having met a better man. I fear how these things may end."

Medea asks further questions as to the manner of his approach, and Ægeus answers : (The herald says) " Two men only accompany him, and about his radiant shoulders

44. Exploits of Theseus

is slung a sword and he has two polished javelins in his hands, and over his fiery locks a well-wrought Laconian helmet, and a purple vest about his chest and a woolly Thessalian cloak. And from his eyes there glistens a ruddy volcanic flame. He is a youth in early manhood, and his thoughts are of the toys of Ares, of war and bronze-smitten battles; and he seeks the splendour-loving Athens."

The list of monsters or robbers whom Theseus over-throws on his journey from Trœzen to Athens varies some-what both in literary versions and upon the vases. A selection appears usually upon Attic vases, joined together into a continuous composition, the hero appearing six times or so in succession, and the limbs of the figures and even of the hero himself often overlapping in the various groups. This appears contrary to the rule usually observed in Greek vase-painting that the same person does not appear more than once in the same scene, to indicate successive actions. But the various actions in this case are really isolated and not consecutive, though they are combined together into a kind of pattern.

If we leave out the Minotaur, which was slain in the Cretan expedition of Theseus, the other exploits, as represented on vases, are usually six : (1) the Bull of Mara-thon, who does not properly belong to the journey from Trœzen ; (2) Sinis the pine-bender, who used to bind his victims to the top of a tree which he bent down and then released ; (3) the Sow of Krommyon, who is usually set side by side with the witch to whom she belonged ; (4) Skiron, who lived on the rocks called by his name, and used to order travellers to wash his feet and then kick them over the cliffs to a giant tortoise below ; (5) Kerkyon, who compelled all travellers to wrestle with him ; (6) Prokrustes, who stretched travellers on his bed, and either cut them short or hammered them out long with his mallet. Periphetes, the club wielder, is also sometimes included, either in addition or instead of one of the others. In the metopes of the Theseum the number is made up to eight by including both the Minotaur and the bull. On the most complete vases, the slaying of the Minotaur is placed inside, and the six exploits just quoted inside or outside the vase. Bacchylides, in his list, gives the first five, including Prokrustes, whom he calls Prokoptas ; but it is difficult to make out whether he means to add as a sixth Polypemon. This passage is obscure, and possibly the text requires amending. Sometimes the slaying of the Minotaur is included in the usual series of exploits ; and it often appears alone in early and black-figured vases.

The description of Theseus' adventurous journey from Trœzen to Athens is little more than an enumeration in Bacchylides ; but the Attic vase-painters had built up a tradition which shows but slight variations in the types chosen to represent the series of exploits. Theseus pulls down the top of the pine-tree of Sinis to bind the robber to it. He charges with sword and chlamys against the Sow of Krommyon behind which the old witch stretches out her arms as if in a magic incantation. Skiron has fallen back upon his rock, while Theseus swings against him the massive bowl which doubtless was to hold the foot-bath, and the gigantic tortoise waits below. Sometimes he seizes Skiron by the leg and hurls him over the cliff. Theseus and Kerkyon are at grips in a wrestling bout. Prokrustes falls back on his own bed, stretching out an arm as if to beg for mercy while Theseus sways the axe with which Prokrustes was in the habit of shortening his victims to fit the bed. The vase-painter selects such subjects and treatment as suit the space he has to fill. Frequently the Minotaur receives separate treatment, either on the inside of a vase which has the usual series outside, or as a subject entirely by itself.

To make up the number of six without the Minotaur, various other exploits might be added. One of these is the Marathonian bull, which, as has already been noticed, does not properly belong to the journey from Trœzen to Athens. Another adversary is Polypemon, sometimes called Korynetes, the club-wielder. His name seems to be included in Bacchylides' list, but in some close relation to Prokrustes (or Prokoptas) which is not easy to understand. Polypemon does not seem to be represented in vases with the exploits of Theseus, though there may be an allusion to him in the club hung up beside the bed of Prokrustes. Nearly all the others that have been mentioned occur on vases, either separately or in various combinations. In many scenes Athena appears as patroness and helper of the hero ; on a vase by Euphronios she actually advances to save him from the bull, which has thrown him to the ground.

When we turn from Bacchylides to Pindar we are at once struck by their different methods of dealing with mythological material. Bacchylides, as we have seen, has an intensely vivid pictorial imagination ; his method is mainly descriptive ; and therefore his work comes much more closely into touch with that of the vase-painter, while Pindar's allusive and ethical treatment of his subjects is more remote, and the lofty splendour of his style does not lend itself so readily to pictorial realisation. And moreover, since the paintings with which we are concerned occur mostly upon Attic vases, they can be compared with the works of Bacchylides the more easily, since the poet had a predilection for Athenian subjects, especially incidents in the life of the Attic hero Theseus, whose name never appears in Pindar, except in two obscure fragments.

There are however some instances in which the words of Pindar and the representation of a scene on vases throw light upon one another. Thus, in describing the overwhelming of the invulnerable Caeneus by the Centaurs, Pindar says " Caeneus, smitten by green pine branches, was lost, cleaving the earth with unbended knee." The meaning of this passage is not easy to understand, until one refers to vase-paintings of the event, in which Caeneus is represented as buried to the waist in the earth, while Centaurs pile rocks and pine branches upon him. The myth of Caeneus, which is discussed by me in J.H.S., XVII., p. 299, need not here be considered in all its aspects. But the best commentary to Pindar's strange expression is to be found in Apollonius Rhodius' Argonautica, I. 57. " Poets sing how Caeneus while yet alive was destroyed

45. Caeneus attacked by Centaurs

by the Centaurs, when he alone drove them before him in his valour. But they turning back to the charge, could not overthrow him nor pierce him, but unbroken and unbent he sank down below the earth, struck by a rushing storm of pine-branches." And in the Orphic Argonautica it is stated that " Caeneus went down alive among the dead beneath the depths of the earth."

The overwhelming of Caeneus with pine-branches and rocks was a favourite subject among vase-painters, both of the black-figured period and of the finest age of Attic vase-painting. Sometimes it appears alone, sometimes as part of a large group of Greeks and Centaurs. It is also found on reliefs, such as those of the Theseum at Athens and those of the temple of Apollo at Bassæ near Phigalia. All alike show the characteristic position of Caeneus, upright but buried to the waist, exactly as Pindar describes him. A common tradition must therefore underlie in this case the work both of the poet and the painter.

In Pindar's close-packed mass of mythological allusions, it is inevitable that many subjects should be touched upon which also find their place upon vases. But as a rule there is not the same scope for comparison between the two versions. And the loftier the theme, the less it lends itself to such comparison. Perhaps as magnificent a passage as any to be found in Pindar is the description of the birth of Athena (VL. VII. 71) : " When by the craft of Hephæstus, by the blow of his axe of beaten bronze Athena sprung forth from the crown of her father's head, and shouted a cry exceeding loud, and the Ocean shuddered at her and Mother Earth." It is impossible to associate this splendid description with the traditional treatment of the theme upon Attic vases, where Athena appears like a little doll issuing from her father's head. But it may well be that the designer of the great pedimental group of the Parthenon, representing the birth of Athena, was inspired more or less directly by the words of Pindar.

In Pindar's description of the strangling of the two serpents by the baby Heracles the scene is described in some detail (Nem. I. 57). The poet tells how after the birth of Heracles and his twin brother, " He did not escape the notice of Hera of the Golden Throne when he was wrapped in saffron swaddling clothes. But the Queen of the gods in hasty anger sent snakes at once. They, when the doors were opened, went into the spacious recess of the chamber, eager to entwine their sharp jaws about the children. But he raised his head upright, and made his first essay of battle, grasping in his two unyielding hands the necks of the two snakes, and in time as they were strangled the breath of life left their terrible limbs. And fear unendurable smote the women that helped the couch of Alcmena. For she herself, starting from her bed on foot unclad, yet strove to ward off the violence of the monsters. And quickly the leaders of the Cadmeans in bronze armour ran in a crowd, and Amphitryon came brandishing his sword unsheathed, smitten with keen distress."

The exceptional amount of vivid description which Pindar gives to this scene may be partly due to the fact that this tale of the infant Heracles and the snakes was a peculiarly Theban legend. It was a common subject in later sculpture and painting ; there was a famous picture of it by Zeuxis, who however belongs to a later generation, and may have been influenced by Pindar. But it is found also upon Attic vases of the early fifth century, and therefore approximately contemporary with the poet. In these the twins are represented upon a short couch, which may be meant for the bed of Alcmena, abridged to suit the available space. Heracles strangles the two snakes with his hands, while his brother Iphicles appeals for help to Alcmena, who in one case starts away in terror, in another has snatched him up in her arms. On the left of the scene Amphitryon rushes up, his sword raised to strike. Behind the couch stands Athena, ready to protect the hero whom she was to help in so many of his subsequent exploits. The representation of the infant Heracles strangling the snakes appears alone upon Theban coins about the middle of the fifth century and the adoption of the same type upon the coins of several Greek cities of a

little later date is probably due to the influence of the
Theban hegemony.[1] The more detailed description in
Theocritus XXIV. differs in no essentials from the version
in Pindar and in the vases, even to the details such as
Iphicles crying out for help and the approach of Alcmena
and Amphitryon. The main difference is that Theocritus
makes the twins ten months old. But Theocritus must
have been acquainted with Zeuxis' picture, which was
probably at Acragas in Sicily.

Out of the other innumerable references to mythology in
Pindar, it is inevitable that there should be many which
allude to tales that also form the subjects of representation upon vases or other works of art. The chariot race
of Pelops and Œnomaus, the prototype of the Olympian
Games, has in Pindar's description a feature which is not
usually found in the artistic tradition. When Pelops
prayed beside the sea to Poseidon for help in his perilous
adventure, the god gave him a team of winged horses
for the race ; and with them he overtook and slew
Œnomaus, and won Hippodamia as his bride. On the
chest of Cypselus, an early Corinthian carving, the chariot
of Pelops in this scene was represented with winged
horses. But as a rule the horses of Pelops, as represented
on vases, are not winged. On the other hand, winged
horses, both separate or yoked to a chariot, are common
in early, especially in orientalising, art. Possibly the
addition of wings to horses and other animals was originally intended to symbolise swiftness. On vases representing Pelops and his bride Hippodamia in a chariot, though
the horses are not winged, they are represented as drawing
the chariot over the sea, indicated by fishes or dolphins.
In some versions of the story the course of the race was
over sea as well as land ; so that the horses, which clearly

[1] P. Gardner, *Types of Greek Coins*, III., 48, VIII., 1, XVI., 6, 7, 8.

are skimming over the waves and not swimming like
Europa's bull, might not inappropriately have been represented as winged. But such was not the tradition of
the vase-painter, though it commended itself to the
imagination of Pindar.

CHAPTER VII

DRAMATIC POETS

I N THE case of the dramatic poets the conditions under which the traditions of poet and artist can be compared differ considerably from those we have so far been considering. In the first place no very rigid line can be drawn between the appeal to the eye and the ear, the space-art and the time-art. For the dramatist has to consider not only the sequence of events and development of character, but also the succession of stage pictures which are presented to the audience ; and these are likely to be influenced not only by the plot in the poet's mind, but also by the traditional form to which both he and his audience are accustomed. It has been said that the scene in a Greek theatre, with its long and narrow stage and its strictly limited number of characters, is like a bas-relief ; and the principles of grouping and composition are much the same for a relief as for a picture.

Before proceeding to compare the poetical and the artistic versions of the various stories, it is necessary to consider the relation between the two in a more general manner. It is evident, in the first place, that the vase-painter or other artist often follows a tradition which is also preserved by the dramatist ; but whether that tradition is borrowed by him from the stage scene is a difficult question, and one that often admits of more than one answer. The examples of vase-paintings that belong to a time earlier than the middle of the fifth century B.C.

have already been considered. But in the case of vase-paintings that are either contemporary with or later than the great works of the Greek drama, it might seem inevitable that these works should influence the versions of the myths given by the vase-painter; and it often is so. But the reproduction of stage settings and characters is not so simple a matter as it is with the modern artist. Suppose, for example, he wishes to represent a scene from one of Shakespeare's plays; the action and dress of the

46. Actors as Birds

characters may not have anything conventionally theatrical about them, but are represented in the dress and surroundings of real life, appropriate to the age and locality with which the play is concerned. The conditions in the Greek theatre are entirely different. The voluminous and conventional tragic dress, with masks and cothurni, is quite unlike anything in real life. And consequently, if a vase-painter or other artist reproduces it in a picture or a relief, he is evidently representing a stage scene, not an alternative version of the same story. Such representations, however, are extremely rare, at least until later times; and even then it is not tragedies or comedies, but rather the quaint burlesques prevalent in South Italy, that offer the commonest subjects. It is true that there are some representations in black-figure style of actors in bird masks and feather dresses that remind us of comic dances ; but these are exceptional and do not seem to tell any story. It may then be asserted, as a general rule, that representations of mythical scenes as they were performed on the stage were not considered by vase-painters as suitable for the exercise of their art –

47. Iphigenia in Tauris

at least until much later times than those with which we are now concerned. On the other hand, we find upon some vases various myths which owe at least their characteristic form to the influence of one of the great Attic dramatists – especially of Euripides, as might have been expected from his popularity and from the frequent revivals of his plays. It therefore is instructive to take an example from a play which we know to have been thus revived, the Iphigenia in Tauris.[1] Certain incidents

[1] Assuming that this play was Iphigenia in Tauris, not in Aulis. See Haigh's *Attic Theatre*, Appendix, B. II.

in this play, such as the handing of a letter to Orestes or to Pylades by Iphigenia, are almost certainly the invention of Euripides. It seems to have been a subject that particularly appealed to him, for it also occurs at the beginning of the Iphigenia in Aulis. On a vase of later, probably South Italian style, this very scene is depicted. Iphigenia, in the richly decorated robes of a priestess, is seen in front of the temple of Artemis in Tauris ; she holds in one hand the key of the temple, with the other she offers a sealed tablet to a youth in travelling costume – cap and chlamys and high boots. Behind him stands another youth leaning on a lustral basin, crowned with a wreath. This must be meant to represent Iphigenia offering to Pylades the letter which he is to carry home to Orestes. The other youth, indicated by the wreath as doomed to sacrifice, must be Orestes, as yet unrecognised by his sister. Above on the right is the goddess Artemis with two javelins and a torch, on the left a young satyr, who probably indicates the wild country in which the scene takes place. The scene on the vase is here evidently taken from the play and may even be regarded as a direct illustration of it. But the figures have no resemblance to actors in the conventional tragic dress ; nor do the surroundings suggest stage scenery. The only thing conventional about them is the shrine occupying the middle of the space on the vase, which is a common feature of South Italian vases, and here is used to represent the temple of the Tauric Artemis.

Another play by Euripides, the Medea, may be compared with the treatment of the same subject upon a large Tarentine amphora. Here the case is not so simple, for the painter attempts to tell the whole story so far as it can be told within his resources. The character and motives of Medea are outside the scope of his art. But the

conventional composition of the Tarentine vase offers
opportunities for bringing together into one scene things
that could hardly have been strictly contemporary. Yet
the narration by a series of scenes in which the same figure
is repeated is here avoided, as is usual in Greek vases.

The interpretation of the Medea vase has been very
various, the main difference between the authorities de-
pending on the question whether the vase picture is

48. Medea

directly dependent on Euripides' play or is based upon a
later play on the same subject but with some different
characters and action. In judging of this matter it is
necessary to make a detailed description of the picture.
In the midst, according to the common practice of Tarentine vases, is a shrine-like structure, here to be identified
as Creon's palace. The moment chosen is after the
children of Medea have carried the poisoned dress to
Creon's daughter, here called Creonteia. She collapses in

Hɢ

agony upon the throne, and Creon is distracted with grief
and pain. In the lower part of the field, to the left, is
Medea threatening one of the children with a sword,
while a young man attempts to rescue the other child.
From the right Jason, carrying sword and spear, advances
towards Medea, but is evidently too late to save the
children. In the centre below, between Jason and Medea,
is a chariot drawn by flying serpents, and driven by a
figure called Oistros (Frenzy). This chariot is clearly the
one in which Medea escaped at the end of the play. But
she could not appear in it at the same time as she was
slaying her children ; and therefore the chariot is driven
not by her, but by an impersonation of the frenzy of
revenge under which she is acting. An analogous impersonation of Madness (Λύττα) appears actually as a character in the *Mad Heracles* of Euripides and on a picture
illustrating the same subject.

So far the composite scene on the vase is in no way
inconsistent with the story as told by Euripides. Though
the painter does not observe the rule recorded by Horace,
" Ne pueros coram populo Medea trucidet," it is hard to
see how he could do so and yet remain intelligible. The
scene is completed by the addition of other figures partly
from the play as we know it, partly from other sources.
The old nurse and the Pædagogus are prominent characters
in the play, and are placed on the vase one on each side of
the central shrine. The indicated escape of one of the
children is inconsistent with the action of the play ; but
an attempt at it is indicated in the play, when the nurse
warns the Pædagogus to keep the children away from
their mother. This attempt is being made by one of the
young men – obviously palace guards – who also supplement the grouping in other directions, for example, in
hastening to the rescue of the fainting princess. At the

extreme right is a figure which has given most support to
those who maintain that another play, varying from that
of Euripides, offers the basis for the picture. For this
figure, in rich oriental dress, has the name written over it –
the ghost of Aëtes. Such a figure has of course no place in
the Euripidean plot : if the vase-painter introduced it of
his own accord, it must have been to emphasise the gap
between Medea's oriental origin and her life in Corinth,
as alluded to more than once in the play. Merope also –
here evidently the mother of the bride – is an introduction
of the vase-painter. Nor does there seem to be any particular appropriateness in the figures who are seated
above as spectators – Athena and Heracles on one side and
the Dioscuri on the other. But such figures are so common
a convention on South Italian vases that they require no
special explanation. The two tripods set upon columns are
probably intended as a kind of acknowledgement that
the scene is borrowed from a theatrical source.

Whether the vase-painting be derived directly from
Euripides' play or from a variation on the same theme by
a later author, it follows a more or less conventional
design which helps the independence of its treatment of
the subject. But as a result it gives a general impression of
the action rather than any sequence of events, so that it
may claim to be in accordance with the traditions of the
artist rather than to follow the literary version in detail.
Dr. Engelmann[1] describes this custom in the introduction
to his book on the relation of vases to the drama. " The
ancient artists," he says, " were far from any attempt to
illustrate the works of their dramatists. And for that
reason they approached their work with greater freedom,
they rounded off their representations by the addition of
figures that were entirely absent from the play, or at least

[1] *Arch. Studien zu den Tragikern*, p. 2.

HG*

had no place in the scenes actually presented ; in short, they sought, in accordance with the principles of their art, which can only recognise extension in space and not in time, to represent the whole as much as possible in all its parts, so as not to give the impression of a single scene, but the representation of the whole." It is true that Dr. Engelmann believes the Medea vase to be derived not from the works of Euripides, but from a play by a later tragedian. But the principles he lays down are most clearly exemplified in this very vase, if the interpretation given above is the right one.

Professor Robert[1] refers to this same vase when he says: " As an example of bold and free extension of myth the Medea vase at Munich may be more closely considered. A mass of new characters and new motives, which are all strange to the Euripidean play, are spread before us by the artist in this composition of many figures ; and yet the scene that he brings before us is none other than that of Euripides ; no other poem, no later revision was before him. He modified it as it had to be modified by an artist familiar with the Euripidean version, but of free design and fancy, who desired to set before our eyes in a single picture the whole vengeance of Medea." Considered from this point of view, the Medea-vase offers an excellent example of the " comprehensive method " in Greek vase-painting.

In the case of the two plays just considered, the Iphigenia and the Medea, we have the advantage of possessing the complete text for comparison with the version given us by the vase-painter. They therefore offer us considerable help in dealing with plays that are only preserved for us in scanty outline or in a disconnected series of extracts and quotations. But before discussing

[1] *Bild und Lied*, p. 37.

such plays it seems advisable to consider another vase-painting which deals with the same story as a well-known play, in this case the Antigone of Sophocles ; and the question is complicated by the fact that Euripides also made a play upon this subject. The main difference in the plot seems to be that while in Sophocles' play Antigone and her lover Hæmon are both killed, in Euripides' version they escape and return after several years with a half-grown child who, as Mæon, continues the dynasty in Thebes. According to this story, Creon seems to have been reconciled to the marriage of Hæmon and Antigone

49. Antigone

by the intervention of Dionysus, perhaps as *deus ex machina*. But there is another version in which this reconciliation is effected by Heracles ; and this last seems to be the one which the vase-painter had in his mind when painting a vase which, both from the subject and from the names inscribed over the figures, evidently refers to the story of Antigone. On this vase, as on the other Apulian vases just mentioned, the centre of the composition is occupied by a small shrine. Within this stands Heracles, apparently addressing Creon, who stands listening to him. On the other side of the shrine is Antigone, with her hands bound behind her, and led by a guard. Behind her on a small eminence stands Hæmon in an attitude of mourning or dejection. Above Creon is Ismene seated, and behind Creon a boy, who must probably be identified as Mæon; he carries a bowl, as if for a sacrifice. It is evident that the vase-painting is derived from the tale of Antigone, but not the Antigone of Sophocles. It has more in common with the Antigone of Euripides, as summarised by Aristophanes the grammarian in the argument to Sophocles' Antigone. But the presence of Heracles instead of Dionysus seems to imply the intervention of a third version, differing from both of the others. The occurrence of all these variants is a warning against too literal inferences as to the plays that suggested the treatment of the story on the vases. It must be remembered that, in addition to the numerous plays of which we have either a summary of the plot or a collection of miscellaneous quotations, there were a great number of which we have no such record. Every year several new plays were produced at the great Dionysiac festivals, not only in Athens, but also in the theatres that existed in many other towns; and though some of these were merely revivals of well-known plays, many of them may have involved a considerable modification both of the plots and the text of such old plays, or may have been an entirely new version of an old story. The two examples just considered, the Medea and the Antigone, suffice to show the problems that arise in such instances.

These conditions and traditions have to be taken into account in any attempt to recover the plots of lost plays by a comparison with the vase-painter's version of the same story. It will be convenient to consider some instances in detail. The tale of Andromeda was the subject of plays by both Sophocles and Euripides, the latter known to us in part from a parody of it in Aristophanes'

Ecclesiasusæ. Several vases represent either scenes from one of these plays or subjects connected with them. One of these vases, in the British Museum, is of the fifth century and therefore approximately contemporary with the plays. There has been some controversy as to the interpretation of this vase. The central part of the action, though not of the composition as a whole, shows three attendants or slaves, of negroid type, employed in fixing two long upright stakes in the ground ; one of them is clearing out a hole in the rocky ground, into which one of his companions drives his stake. Beyond this group on the right side are two more figures, an oriental king, distinguished by his tiara, seated on a rock in an attitude of dejection, and Perseus standing behind him, raising his hand to his forehead as if in grief or anxiety ; the winged cap identifies him sufficiently, though he does not, as in other representations of the same subject, carry the harpe or wear winged sandals. At the other end of the scene are three more Ethiopian attendants, carrying a chest and vases, such as were appropriately offered at tombs ; one of them carries a stool. Between these two groups is another which forms the centre of the whole composition. It consists of a figure facing, supported or led by two negro slaves, and with its arms round the necks of these slaves. The drapery of the central figure is remarkable ; on its head is a tiara like that of the king, and it wears richly embroidered tunic and leggings, thus having a somewhat amazonian appearance. There has been some dispute about the identification of this figure. Professor Petersen[1] suggested that it was the unworthy suitor of Andromeda, an oriental prince who left her to her fate, and is characterised here by his effeminate attitude. But there does not seem to be any reason to suppose that this character had

[1] J.H.S. XXIV., p. 99.

we have seen already, in the version made by Stesichorus. In any case, these scenes cannot have originated from the Æschylean version; for the Orestean trilogy was not performed until 458 B.C., and several of the vases just quoted are shown by their style to belong at latest to the early years of the fifth century. On the other hand some

51. Orestes purified by Apollo

vases of later period represent events in the story which differ from the plays of Æschylus – especially the purification of Orestes by Apollo from the pollution of his matricide, though this is not necessarily inconsistent with his legal acquittal by the Areopagus. Another vase follows pretty closely the opening scene of the Eumenides, with Orestes taking refuge at the Delphic Omphalos, and Apollo saving him from the Eumenides who sleep around

him. The main difference in this scene is the presence of
Athena, to whose help he was to appeal at Athens ; but it
was in accordance with the custom of the vase-painter
that her favour should thus be implied.

CHAPTER VIII

HELLENISTIC ART

S O FAR we have been mainly concerned with the alternative versions of Greek myths by the poet and the vase-painter, each following the traditions of his own art. But after the time of Alexander the work of the vase-painter fails us almost entirely. On the other hand we find not infrequently in the Hellenistic poets elaborate and detailed descriptions of works of art such as suit the taste of a critical age. Such descriptions are not indeed unknown in earlier Greek times ; the instances that at once occur to us are the Homeric Shield of Achilles and the Hesiodic Shield of Heracles. These however differ from the representations we have so far been considering in several respects. For the most part they do not represent a story or an event, but rather the ordinary happenings of life in town and country. Such at least is the case with the shield of Achilles ; and though there are some recollections of myths on the Hesiodic shield – such as Perseus flying from the Gorgons or the battle of Greeks and Centaurs, there is no attempt to include or summarise a whole story. On the other hand, these descriptions do apply to scenes or technique familiar to the poet and to his hearers, and both poet and audience are probably more interested in the objects described than in the skill or liveliness of the description.

There are some instances earlier than the Hellenistic

age of descriptions of works of art ; a good example is
offered by the description given in Euripides' Ion of the
woven stuffs hung up by Ion to make a tent ; but in this
case the ornamentation is expressly said to be of oriental,
or " barbarous," character, for it was the spoil from the
Amazons dedicated by Heracles.   The subjects are
" Heaven assembling the stars in the circle of Ether ;' the
Sun driving his horses to his last flame, drawing after him
the bright light of Hesperus.   And dark-robed Night
guided her car with yokes and no traces ; and the Stars
escorted the goddess."   Then come other constellations
" and the light-bearing Dawn pursuing the stars."

A comparison at once suggests itself here with the
well-known Blacas vase in the British Museum which

52. Sunrise (Blacas Vase)

represents the sunrise in the form of anthropomorphic
imagination.   Here the sun rises over the waves in his
four-horse chariot, and before him the stars – in the form
of boys – take headers or dive into the water. He is
preceded by the Dawn-goddess, who is winged and advances over a hill in pursuit of Cephalus ; and further in
front Night, seated upon a horse, sinks behind some rocks.
It is possible to regard this as a mere setting for the myth
of Cephalus and the Dawn-goddess, with the rising sun
and setting moon as a kind of frame to the picture, as in
the east pediment of the Parthenon and several other

recorded compositions. But the general impression given by the vase is rather of an allegorical or impersonating representation of the sunrise, in which Cephalus is merely an incident.

As an example of an elaborate description of a work of art after the Alexandrian manner we may take the cloak, the gift of Athena, which Jason wore when he went to see Hypsipyle, the Queen of Lemnos. After mentioning the brilliance of its red and purple colour, various mythical scenes are described.[1] "In it were the Cyclopes seated at their eternal task forging a thunderbolt for lord Zeus; it was partly fashioned and shining, but there was still one ray wanting, which they were beating with iron hammers, glowing with the heat of fierce fire. And in it were the two sons of Antiope, daughter of Asopus, Amphion and Zethus. And Thebes lay close by yet unfortified, of which they were but now laying the foundation stones. Zethus was raising on his shoulders the summits of rocky mountains, as if with toil; and Amphion came after him playing on his golden lyre, and a rock twice as large followed his footsteps. And next in the decoration was the deep-tressed Cytherea, holding the bronze shield of Ares; and from her shoulders the clasp of her dress was loosened under the left breast; and her reflection could be seen clearly in the bronze shield. And in it was a shaggy herd of cattle; and for the cattle the Teleboiæ and the sons of Electryon were fighting, the ones in defence, and the others wishing to drive them, the Taphian robbers; and the dewy meadow was wet with blood, and their numbers overcame the few herdsmen. And in it two chariots were wrought in strife. Pelops drove the first, shaking the reins, and beside him was Hippodamia; and racing after them Myrtilus drove his team, and with him Oenomaus,

[1] *Apoll. Rhod. Argonautica*, I. 730–768.

grasping his spear in his hand and reaching out, fell as the axle was broken on the nave, eager to strike Pelops in the back. And in it was Phœbus Apollo, yet a boy, shooting great Tityus, as he boldly dragged his mother by her cloak, Tityus whom Elera bore and Earth brought up to a second birth. And in it was Phrixus the Minyan listening to the ram which seemed as if to speak. When you saw them you would keep silence, and deceive your mind, expecting to hear from them some speech ; you might look on them long in this expectation. Such were the gifts of the goddess, Athena Tritonis.''

This list of subjects seems to have no very obvious connection with the context, except in the case of Phrixus and the ram. The rest seems a more or less random collection from a mythological dictionary. But it is not difficult to find examples of them in Greek art, either earlier or later.

For our present purpose it is not necessary to draw any strong distinction between Alexandrian or Hellenistic and Roman poets and artists. Catullus, for example, gives a detailed description of a piece of tapestry used as a bed-spread at the nuptials of Peleus and Thetis. This is expressly stated to be decorated with ancient designs. On it were represented the desertion of Ariadne by Theseus ; and incidentally the whole story of Theseus and the Minotaur is told, ending with the entry of Bacchus and his route of Satyrs and Mænads, the whole being nearly as long as the poem on Peleus and Thetis in which it is set. But the episode of Ariadne and Theseus is not so much a narrative of events as a succession of pictures. We should expect a learned poet such as Virgil to refer to works of art. His famous description of the death of Laocoön must be reserved for separate consideration. But there are other passages in which the poet expressly

Romulus to Augustus, including the most stirring and picturesque events, so that when he had received the shield Æneas " bore upon his shoulder the glorious destiny of his descendants."

It is not clear how far Virgil realised in detail the composition of the shield and the relation of the various scenes of which it is composed. An indication seems to be given when he says that the representation of Manlius defending the Capitol against the attack of the Gauls was placed *in summo*, at the top ; but some commentators think this simply means that Manlius stood on the top of the rock. Occasional bits of technical description, such as the silver geese of the Capitol and the gold hair and torques of the Gauls, serve to remind us that the description is of a work of art. But the interest of poet and reader alike is in the historical events rather than in their artistic form.

A discussion of the description of works of art by Virgil can hardly avoid some consideration of the description of the death of Laocoön, especially in relation to the well-known group of the same subject. It is true that the description in Virgil cannot be regarded as derived from a work of art ; nor on the other hand can the sculptural group be regarded as an illustration to Virgil. There has been much discussion among earlier critics and archæologists as to which of the two is the earlier ; but fortunately it is now possible to put the chronological basis for this discussion on solid foundations.

Pliny tells us that the sculptors who made the Laocoön were Agesander, Polydorus, and Athenodorus. It is shown by inscriptions that they belonged to a well-known family of artists, and were working about the middle of the first century B.C. in Rhodes. They cannot therefore have been acquainted with Virgil's poem, which was not published until after his death in 19 B.C. ; nor, on the other hand, is it likely that the poet could have seen the group, which probably was not removed from Rhodes to Rome until a later date, when it was placed in the Baths of Titus. In all probability the two versions of the story are entirely independent of each other, except in so far as they both deal with the same myth. But this fact does not affect the soundness of Lessing's criticism in general, or the distinction he draws between the appeal to the ear, with its possible extension in time, and the effect to the eye, with its possible extension in space.

Let us now compare the two versions. Virgil first tells us how Laocoön, with the proverbial words " timeo Danaos et dona ferentes," launched a spear against the wooden horse. After this, as he was sacrificing to Neptune, we have first a long description of the terrible approach of the two snakes from Tenedos across the sea. " Then first the two snakes wind themselves about the little bodies of his two sons, and bite and feed upon their limbs. Then (*Post*) they seize on the father, as he rushes to their aid with a weapon, and bind him in mighty coils ; they entwine twice about his waist, twice about his neck their scaly bodies, and tower head and neck above him. He tries with his hand to loosen their coils, the black venom sprinkling his priestly fillets. His terrible shrieks ascend to heaven." Then the snakes slip away and disappear beneath the shield of the goddess. The impression here conveyed is that the children are enveloped and slain before the father, who comes to their aid, is attacked. It is hardly conceivable that the three could in such a sequence of events be drawn together into such a group as we see in the sculpture. This would be no proof that neither version was known to the authors of the other, if such knowledge were otherwise probable. The sculptors gain their effect by the skilful combination of these struggling elements into a harmonious group, so that the pain and horror of its detail is made tolerable, if not pleasing, by the unity and completeness of the whole. The poet's felicity of language and beauty of verse reconcile us to the horror of his narrative ; the monstrous nature of the snakes is dwelt upon ; but so far as we have picturesque realisation of the scene at various points in the action, it is totally different from that which appealed to the sculptor.

The means of expression and representation, whether addressed to the eye or the ear, shows a varied but continuous development, from the crude experiments of primitive times to the highly developed attainments of the poet and the artist in classical times. The two some- times work independently, sometimes in close relation to each other, sometimes with not very successful invasion of each other's provinces. Aristotle says, " Ὕλῃ καὶ τρόποις μιμήσεως διαφέρουσι " (" they differ in the material and manner of their imitation "), and Lessing adds, " The first man to compare painting and poetry with each other was a man of fine feelings, who was aware of a similar effect of both arts upon himself. Both, he felt, transform things absent to present, appearance to reality ; both deceive us and the deception of both is pleasing."